SLOOPS & SHALLOPS

Sloops & Shallops

By
WILLIAM A. BAKER

Illustrations by the Author

University of South Carolina Press

This edition published in Columbia, S.C.,
by the University of South Carolina Press

Manufactured in the United States of America

Library of Congress Cataloging-in-Publication Data

Baker, William A.
  Sloops & shallops.

  (Classics in maritime history)
  Reprint. Originally published: Barre Pub. Co., 1966.
  1. Sloops. 2. Navigation–United States. 3. United
States–History, Naval. I. Title. II. Title: Sloops
and shallops. III. Series.
VM311.F7B3 1987   387.2'2   87–16167
ISBN 0–87249–538–8

PREFACE

IN VIEW of all the references to sloops in American colonial records, readers of my earlier book *Colonial Vessels* may have wondered why the sloop was not included. They also may have wondered why Chapter II of that book—"Concerning Shallops" — did little more than document the characteristics of one particular seventeenth-century shallop, that carried on *Mayflower* in 1620. Both sloop and shallop derived from the same Germanic word hence confusion in their use was inevitable. Some of this confusion may never be dispelled but in the following pages I have attempted to trace the development of the sloops and shallops employed along the east coast of North America from the days of the early settlers through the first quarter of the nineteenth century. The characteristics of sloop-rigged vessels during the remainder of the nineteenth century to the practical end of commercial sail in the present century have been covered in magazine articles and books by several authors.

As in all work of this type I am indebted to previous researchers and to the patient transcribers of musty court records. Their names will be found in the footnotes. In particular, however, I must thank Mr. M. V. Brewington, Assistant Director of the Peabody Museum, Salem, Massachusetts, for the use of his notes on the early shipping of Maryland and Virginia and Mr. H. I. Chapelle, Curator in Charge, Division of Transportation, Smithsonian Institution, Washington, D.C. for the use of his model take-offs and notes on the St. John woodboats. My thanks also go to the editors of "The American Neptune" for permission to use my material on the packet sloop *Mayflower* which first appeared in that journal.

My final thanks go to my wife for her invaluable aid in collecting notes, typing the manuscript, and providing non-technical advice in order that non-technical readers might better follow my course.   W.A.B.

LIST OF ILLUSTRATIONS

TABLE OF CONTENTS

PROLOGUE

TO THE question "What is the most typical American sailing vessel?" the answer is generally "The schooner, of course!" But the sloop appeared on the American scene some seventy-five years before the word schooner became part of our sea-going language. Such are the whims of fate that the schooner is now a *rara avis* in North America and what is now defined as a sloop forms a major portion of our sailing yacht fleets and of the last commercial sailing fleet, the oyster dredgers of Chesapeake Bay. Curiously though, what today is called a schooner according to the present method of classification by rig alone, may well have been known to the seafaring population when it first appeared as a sloop.

E. van Konijnenburg, in discussing the development of various types of sailing vessels in the Netherlands, points out several times in the course of his treatise that there has seldom been a radical invention of a vessel type.[1] The use of a new name did not mean the introduction of a completely new type. At a given period in the maritime history of any country there have existed a number of vessel types suitable for certain pursuits — deep-sea and coastwise cargo carrying, deep-sea and coastal fishing, and cargo-carrying and fishing on inland waters were the main uses. Changes in vessels for such employment occurred but slowly. They were the result of different trade routes, the silting up of ports, the change in manner of fishing, and improved technology which permitted different methods of construction.

Perhaps many more changes, however, were the result of mere whim — the inevitable trait of builders and artists to try something a little different. The addition or change of a given feature on vessels for a certain service, if successful over a period of time, usually resulted in a new type name to differentiate the newer from the older boats. To the merchants and seamen changes in type names probably meant little. Until the middle of the nineteenth century vessels were known primarily by hull type or service rather than by rig. Since then, for various reasons, writers in England and the United States have classed vessels almost solely by rig. One can just imagine a marine researcher of a few centuries hence trying to define the American schooner — two to seven masts, wide and shoal, narrow and deep, a fishing vessel with the characteristics of a pleasure boat, and so on. By comparison, a European type name, even down to the last days of sail, was a fairly good indication of hull capabilities.

Sloep in Dutch, slup in Swedish, chaloupe in French, and shallop in English — but just what was it? This question was posed at the beginning of my "Notes on a Shallop" that first appeared in 1957.[2] To the list of equivalents may be added the German schlup, and the Basque, Portuguese, and Spanish chalupa. Most authorities agree that all versions are derived from the Dutch sloep. "Notes on a Shallop" endeavored to answer the question for the reconstruction of a specific shallop — that carried on *Mayflower* in 1620 for use by the band of colonists who eventually settled at what is now Plymouth, Massachusetts. There is, however, far more to the story of shallops and sloops.

The terms shallop and sloop are widely employed in the maritime records of seventeenth-century North America but it is likely a mistake to assume that there was always a clear line of demarcation. The word shallop apparently made its appearance in the written English language in the account

of Martin Frobisher's 1576 voyage from England in search
of the Northwest Passage to China. Christopher Hall, master
of the bark *Gabriel*, wrote concerning the boats of the Eski-
mos — "Their boates are made all of Seales skinnes, with a
keele of wood within the skin: the proportion of them is like
a Spanish shallop, save only they be flat in the bottom, and
sharpe at both ends".[3] Such a comment indicates that, in
spite of this probably being the first written use of the term
shallop in English, the Spanish shallop was a type of small
craft well-known to English seamen of the late sixteenth century. An early English spelling was "shalloop", an obvious
attempt to render the French word phonetically.

In Hakluyt's "Voyages" we can find many references
to various small craft — just plain boats, cockboats, long-
boats, shipboats, skiffs, light horsemen, shallops, and rowing
pinnaces. John White's account of his voyage to the West
Indies and Virginia in 1590 records the putting to sea on 20
March of three ships "with two small Shallops". Although
called small they were apparently too big to be carried conveniently aboard any of the three ships, for on — "the 25 at
midnight both our Shallops were sunke being towed at the
ships stearnes by the Boatswaines negligence". On 1 April
he continued — " . . . we ankored in Santa Cruz rode, where
we found two great shippes of London lading in Sugar, of
whom we had 2 shipboats to supply the losse of our Shallops".[4] In this case the shallops had qualities especially suitable for an expedition but boats carried for odinary ship services, which can be assumed were less satisfactory, had to
suffice. Specifically mentioned in 1597 are the shallops of
the French and Basque fishermen in the waters off Cape Breton Island and Newfoundland. Two English ships from

London put into a Newfoundland harbor to obtain some shallops but could find none.[5]

Not only do we have these and similar accounts of the use of shallops by early explorers but from unknown expeditions or perhaps fishermen the natives in the New England region of North America obtained shallops. Two accounts of Bartholomew Gosnold's voyage along the New England coast in 1602 mention a shallop seen off what is now New Hampshire. Gabriel Archer, a "gentleman" on Gosnold's bark *Concord* noted — "From the said Rocke, came towards us a Biscay shallop with saile and Oares, having eight persons in it, . . . approching us neere, wee perceived then to be Savages . . . One that seemed to be their Commander wore a Wastecote of blacke worke, a paire of Breeches, cloth Stockings, Shoes, Hat, and Band, one or two more had also a few things made by some Christians, these with a piece of Chalke described the Coast thereabouts, and could name Placentia of the New-found-land, . . . ".[6] John Brereton, one of the crew on *Concord*, referred to the same craft as a Basque shallop. The reference to Placentia might be taken as an indication that a Biscay or Basque shallop was sufficiently seaworthy to make the passage from Placentia to New Hampshire.

William Strachey, writing of the Sagadahoc colony of 1607 at the mouth of the Kennebec, referred twice to natives in shallops — once in a Spanish shallop and again in a Biscay shallop.[7] Robert Juet, mate on Henry Hudson's *Half Moon* in 1609, reported — "Then wee espied two French shallops full of Countrey People come into the Harbour, . . . ".[8] This encounter is assumed to have been in the Penobscot Bay region. A Jesuit report of 1611 definitely places a shallop in the Penobscot; it might have been one of those previously seen by *Half Moon*'s crew.[9] As Juet mentioned — "a great

Fleet of French-men, which lay Fishing on the Banke; . . . "
this near the southern tip of Nova Scotia, a possible source
of the French shallops is apparent.

These few references are sufficient to indicate the existence of a well-known small craft whose home waters were in
the Bay of Biscay but which was probably employed generally around the Iberian peninsula. It was a fairly sizable
craft with enough distinguishing features to take it out of the
plain "boat" category. Its distinguishing features were also
such as to make it particularly desirable for exploring expeditions and for fishing operations. It was admired and widely
adopted along the Atlantic coast of France, in Cornwall
through connections with Brittany, and in the Netherlands.
Like many small craft it so developed through the years that
the later craft to be described as shallops would have been
unrecognizable to early seventeenth-century seamen.

❀❀❀❀❀❀❀❀❀❀❀❀❀❀❀❀❀❀❀❀❀❀❀❀❀❀❀❀❀❀❀❀❀

CHAPTER I

Early   Shallops

IT WAS common practice for sixteenth-century explorers
to carry on their ships, in addition to the normal complement of boats, a shallop or some other type of small craft in
pieces ready to be assembled upon arrival at their base of
operations — "chaloupe en fagot" as the French termed it.
As the majority of the ships employed for exploration were
relatively small this practice permitted the carriage of a larger
boat than otherwise could have been accommodated. The
first shallop used by the colonists of the first permanent settlement in what is now the United States was just such a
"chaloupe en fagot". Captain John Smith recorded the arrival
of the Virginia Company colonists off Cape Henry at the
mouth of Chesapeake Bay in 1607 and continued — ". . . so
next day we began to build our shallop, which had been shipped in portions, easy to be fitted together".[1] This "next day"
was 27 April 1607 and the completed shallop was launched
on 18 May after which Smith and some of the gentlemen went
in her up what is now the James River. Smith's map of Chesapeake Bay shows a single-masted double-ended boat, presumably this shallop, in one of the upper reaches of the Bay.

In general the colonists who settled at Jamestown in

1

Virginia were gentlemen adventurers with little taste for or interest in fishing and other seafaring activities. As one result the colony's records of boatbuilding and shipbuilding activities prior to 1612 are so varied that no accurate statement can be made concerning the number and types of vessels. A 12- or 13-ton vessel of an unknown type was constructed before 1611 but in the same year Lord De La Warr reported to the Council of the Virginia Company in London that there were but two boats and one barge in the whole colony.[2] One explanation for the lack of boats might be that the most easily available craft, the Indian dugout canoes, were employed in what little local fishing was done.

In 1612 Samuel Argall — later Sir Samuel — arrived at Jamestown on 17 September in his ship *Treasurer* and from then until the first of November his time was spent — " . . . helping to repair such ships and Boats, as I found heere decayed for lacke of Pitch and Tarre . . . . ". Later in the month he fitted his ship for the carriage of corn and sailed to the Indian village of Patowomeck on the Pembroke River, now the Rappahannock. In order to transport the corn, 1100 bushels, from the village to his ship he built a "stout shallop". Among other pursuits he and his men built a "frigat" and a fishing boat. In May 1613 Argall and some of his crew used the new shallop for an exploring expedition along the eastern shore of Chesapeake Bay.[3]

Following Argall's activities the Virginia records continued in a confused state, for in 1619 when Sir Thomas Smith ended his term as Treasurer of the Company his opponents charged that there were in the colony only one shallop, one ship's boat, two privately owned small boats, and one old frigate belonging to Bermuda.[4] A supporter of Smith claimed, however, that barks, pinnaces, shallops, barges, and other boats had been built. Similar charges were exchanged by others in 1621 and 1623. Although undoubtedly there had been from time to time in the colony carpenters capable of building boats, those in charge of the colony continually asked the Company officials in London for trained ship-wrights. They had no success until 1622.

Among the passengers who arrived on the ship *Abigail* in the middle of 1622 was Captain Thomas Barwick with twenty five men trained in boat- and shipbuilding. After constructing houses for themselves at Jamestown they started building shallops, considered the best type of small craft for transporting tobacco, which by then had become the colony's major export, from shore to ship. This project soon failed as nearly all who had arrived on *Abigail* including Captain Barwick and many others died of a contagious dis-ease. Boat building undoubtedly continued in a small way and boats may have been obtained from visiting ships, for when Virginia became a Crown Colony there were thirty-eight boats, two shallops, one bark, one skiff, and one canoe listed in the census made in January 1625. There were prob-ably more, as many plantations failed to list their small craft. The skiff, the bark, and a 4-ton shallop were among ten small craft reported by Jamestown.[5]

From 1625 on for about the next one hundred years there are all sorts of references to shallops in Virginia. The majority are in court records but there are some in private journals, and, at the end of the period, in newspapers. The number of references decreases with the passing of time as other types of small craft were developed to suit local con-ditions.

Boatbuilding began in what is now Maryland at the fur trading post established on Kent Island in 1631 by Cap-tain William Claiborne, a partner and the American agent of Clobery & Company of London. The shallop *Firefly* was built there in 1631; the next year her sides were raised and she was decked for half her length.[6] Before 1635 she was followed by a wherry, the shallop *Star*, which was manned by a crew of four or five when trading with the Indians, the shallop *Cockatrice* which had a crew of fourteen, and the pinnace *Long Tail*.[7] Another fur trader, Captain Henry Fleet, built a shallop in 1632 while he was with the Indians.[8]

In 1634 the proprietary colony of Cecilius Calvert, Lord Baltimore, was established on the site of an Indian village near the mouth of the Potomac River. About two hundred settlers arrived on the ship *Ark* and the pinnace *Dove* bringing with them on *Ark* a shallop. This shallop was apparently carried whole for soon after the vessels dropped their anchors the women servants were put into her to wash the voyagers' dirty clothes. With a number of women leaning over the side, piles of wet clothes, and undoubtedly plenty of water sloshing around one can easily imagine the result. The shallop did capsize but after a hectic few minutes all the servants were saved from drowning.[9] The settlers also brought "en fagot" a craft described as a barge for which they had separate planks and ribs.

The building and use of shallops as well as of other types of small craft spread in Maryland as previously in Virginia. From the Maryland court records and the proceedings of the Council we can find that shallops were employed for loading and unloading ships, for trading voyages around Chesapeake Bay, for military expeditions against the Indians, and in actions between the settlers at St. Marys — this was the seat of Lord Baltimore's government — and the traders on Kent Island. A shallop served as the first recorded pilot boat in the colony.[10] There are a few references to shallops used for fishing but as in Virginia the early economy of Maryland was based upon tobacco and the shallop for a considerable period proved the most convenient type for transporting casks of that commodity.

Although included in "Notes on a Shallop" it will be best for a connected account to repeat here information concerning the shallop brought to New England on *Mayflower* in 1620. A pamphlet published in London in 1622 stated: "Munday the thirteenth of November, we unshipped our Shallop, and drew her on land, to mend and repaire her, having bin forced to cut her downe in bestowing her betwixt the decks, and she was much opened with the peoples lying in her, which kept us long there (at Provincetown), for it was sixteene or seventeene daies before the Carpenter had finished her: . . . . ".[11]

In his journal *Of Plimouth Plantation* Governor William Bradford covered the same subject with the following: " . . . they having brought a large shalop with them out of England, stowed in quarters in ye ship, they now gott her out & sett their carpenters to worke to trime her up; but being much brused and shatered in ye shipe with foule weather, they saw she would be longe in mending".[12]

The exact method of carrying this shallop on *Mayflower* has been the subject of much speculation. The term "quarters" leads one to assume that Bradford meant that the shallop was cut into four pieces for convenient storage. It seems more likely, however, that a number of planks on each side and the upper parts of the shallop's ribs were removed. The use of "quarters" to mean living accommodations dates from 1594 so Bradford probably was specifying a location and not a condition.

While the shallop was being repaired the ship's longboat served to transport the colonists to shore where the women were able to do their washing under more stable circumstances than the women of Maryland. While some of

the men went off exploring others were employed in search-
ing out suitable trees and sawing timber for another shallop.[13]
By the spring of 1623, however, only one shallop was left in
the Plymouth colony and because of low stocks of food she
was employed continually for fishing. The men of the colony
were divided into crews of six or seven each and as soon as
one crew returned in the shallop another took her to sea
again.[14] In 1624 a ship-carpenter arrived on *Charity* and
according to Bradford: ". . . he quickly builte them 2 very
good & strong shalops (which after did them greate service), and a great and strong lighter, and had hewne timber
for 2 catches; but that was lost, for he fell into a feaver in ye
hote season of ye year, and though he had the best means ye
place could afford, yet he dyed; . . . ".[15]

Thus this boatbuilding venture in the Plymouth colony
suffered the same fate as Jamestown's a year earlier. The
colony did, however, have some men with boatbuilding skills
as in 1626 the biggest shallop was sawn in two, lengthened
five or six feet, made deeper by the addition of planks on the
sides, and fitted with a deck.[16] In the next year a pinnace
was built at the head of Buzzards Bay for trading to the
southward.[17] Although not definitely stated it is probable
that men capable of such operations could and did build shallops and small boats.

Upon the failure of a fishing settlement on Cape Ann
a group of emigrants moved from there in 1626 to the site
of the present Salem in Massachusetts. Additional settlers
arrived in 1628 and by the end of 1629 Salem men had occupied a point in what is now Boston harbor. These settlements
came within the grant of the corporation that operated under
the title of "The Governor and the Company of the Massachusetts Bay in New England". Unlike the governing bodies
of Virginia and Maryland this company early made provi-

sions for boat- and shipbuilding and fishing In a general letter of instructions dated 17 April 1629 there is reference to six shipwrights and six fishermen sent over[18] and another letter dated 28 May 1629 records the sending of " . . . The provisions for building of shipps as Pitch, Tarr, Rozen, Okum old ropes for Okum, Cordage & Salycloth . . . . with 9 fferkins and 5 halfe barrells of Nayles . . . ". The latter also noted "but soe soone as 3 shallops shalbe finished, two of them to bee sett out for the Companie, . . . and one for our Governor & his partners, . . . "[19] and continued with details pertaining to fishing and the equipment supplied. The planting of tobacco ". . . unless it bee some small quantitie for meere necessitie and for Phisick for preservation of their healths, . . ." was specifically forbidden within the Bay Colony.[20]

The need for housing occupied the shipwrights and it is not known just when they were able to be employed for the purpose for which they were sent. John Winthrop in *Arbella*, flagship of the fleet that carried more settlers for the Boston harbor region, reported considerable activity off the New Engand coast in 1630. On Friday, 11 June, he wrote that they were two leagues from the Isles of Shoals where they could see a ship riding at anchor and five or six shallops under sail. Later they met another shallop belonging to some English fishermen which was sailing from Cape Ann to the Isles of Shoals. The next morning, when south of Cape Ann near Bakers Island, *Arbella* was boarded by Isaac Allerton of Plymouth who was en route to Pemaquid in a shallop and another shallop from Salem served to pilot the ship to an anchorage to the westward of Bakers Island.[21]

The preceding material establishes the wide use of shallops in the early days of the North American colonies but we must now try to define its form and rig. To confuse matters, however, the term shallop seems to have been used quite early and particularly by the Spanish in much the same manner as pinnace and sloop were later employed — as an indication of use or rating rather than type. Henry VIII of England in 1542 procured in Spain two "zabras" or pinnaces which were employed as dispatch vessels to carry his correspondence with the Spanish emperor. One of these vessels was sometimes referred to as the "Spanish shallop".[22] In 1552 there were six shallops in an English fleet sent out against pirates.[23]

In 1565 several chalupas sailed from Spain for the New World settlements in the capacity of transports carrying troops, munitions, and provisions in company with at least one large galleon. Three of the chalupas completed the voyage — one of 75, one of 70, and one of 60 toneladas — but lost their foremasts in a storm. The 70-tonelada chalupa had a crew of 15, carried 83 soldiers, and was armed with one bronze gun.[24] Based on Spanish tonnage rules of the period she might have been about 64 feet long on deck with a breadth of about 17½ feet and a depth of 7¼ feet. Not very big for 98 persons plus their food and drink along with some cargo, but such a chalupa is hardly the sort of craft described by our various colonial references.

Much more useful for our purpose is a book in Spanish that contains the earliest known printed plans for ships and what is probably the first marine dictionary published in any language — the *Instruction Nauthica* of Doctor Diego Garcia de Palacio printed in Mexico City in 1587. This work set the pattern for later printed descriptions by stating that every ship needed a "batel" — boat — to serve it by performing such duties as placing and recovering anchors, loading and unloading cargo, and towing in and out of port. Each ship also had a "chalupa" which was three-quarters of the batel in length and breadth. Both the batel and the chalupa were double- enders, bluffer in the bow than at the stern, but the chalupa was more finely modelled than the batel. Both were equipped with sheaves at the stem and windlasses for use in recovering anchors. The sizes of the batel and chalupa theoretically varied from ship to ship as the length of the batel was determined by the space available for carrying it on a ship's deck.

Although the *Instruction Nauthica* has no drawings of the batel or chalupa a Portuguese manuscript on shipbuilding compiled in 1616 by Manuel Fernandez has drawings of two batels. The shapes of these confirm the above description — fuller forward than aft — and an outline drawing of the one intended for use as a ship's boat is shown in Figure 1. This batel has a straight sternpost but the other, which is even fuller forward, has a curved sternpost. The position of one mast practically amidship is shown but the shaded reproduction from which the drawing was made is so dark that it is impossible to tell whether there is another step forward. Pictorial evidence from about 1546 to 1637 indicates that the English employed boats of the same general shape.

It is interesting to note that English records concerning the travels of Henry, Earl of Derby, from 1390 to 1393 contain many references to batellas employed to carry people from ship to shore and to tow large ships out of harbors.[25] Portuguese influence in the East shows in the type names of an Arabian vessel in the Persian Gulf and two coasters in Indian waters. The Arabian batel is a double-ended vessel formerly employed widely for pearl fishing and piratical ventures. The two Indian vessels — the batella and batil — now have small transom sterns but originally may have been double-enders too.[26]

For an English definition of a shallop let us turn to the earliest English marine dictionary, Sir Henry Mainwaring's *The Seaman's Dictionary* which is believed to have been com-

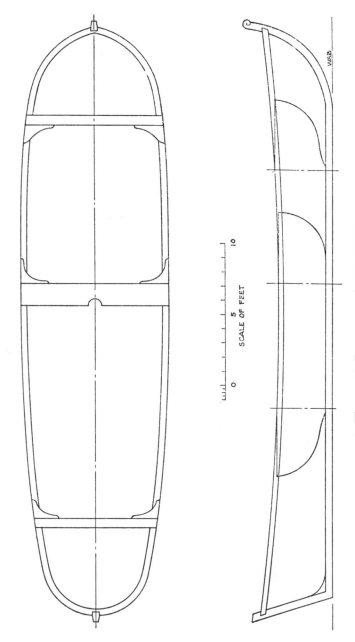

SCALE OF FEET

0 5 10

Figure 1. Portuguese batel, 1616.

piled between 1620 and 1623 but not printed until 1644. Unfortunately, the word "shallop" is not listed, but under "boat" is the following: "The boat belonging to a ship is either called the ship's boat or the long boat, and this is ever intended to be able to carry forth and weigh her sheet anchor. Other small boats which they carry for lightness to hoist in and out quickly, are called skiffs or shallops, according to their form. A good long boat will live in any grown sea if the water be sometimes freed, unless the sea break very much. The rope by which it is towed at the ship's stern is called the boat rope, . . . A ship's boat is the very model of a ship and is built with parts in all things answerable to those which a ship requires, both for sailing and bearing a sail, . . . ".[27]

Under "skiff" Mainwaring simply refers back to "boat" but Nathaniel Boteler in his *A Dialogicall Discourse Concerning Marine Affairs* of 1634, the technical portion of which was taken largely from Mainwaring, stated: "It (the skiff or shallop) is a smaller and lighter and so a nimbler boat than the long-boat, and the peculiar employment of it is to row speedily upon all occasions, from one place or ship to another; and this boat may also with more safety and convenience be brought to the ship's side, when the ship is at sea and the billows anything high, than the long-boat can".[28]

My "Notes on a Shallop" stated that from Mainwaring we find that "*form* has something to do with defining a shallop although it has not been possible to determine just how". Based on the description in the *Instrucion Nauthica* and the pictorial evidence of the 1616 Portuguese manuscript which has a drawing of a skiff — esquife — there is now no question but that the form of the stern determined the basic difference between a skiff and a shallop. The former had a square stern while the latter was a double-ender.

Although the *Instrucion Nauthica* gives a definite size

relation between the long-boat and the shallop such may not have been actual practice on Spanish vessels and certainly was not on English ships. Early in 1627 *Prince Royal*, a 1200-ton ship, had a long-boat with a length of 51 feet, a breadth of 11 feet, and a depth of 3 feet 10 inches. Her shallop was 27 feet long, 6 feet 9 inches wide, and 2 feet 4 inches deep. The long-boat of the 732-ton *Bear* was 41 feet long, 11 feet 7 inches wide, and 3 feet 10 inches deep while her second boat, a rowing pinnace which would have had a square stern, had a length of 28 feet, a breadth of 7 feet, and a depth of 2 feet 8 inches.[29] Oppenheim, referring to British naval practice of about 1650, wrote: " . . . The long boat was apparently still towed astern; it invariably was in 1625, since the Cadiz fleet of that year lost every long boat in crossing the Bay of Biscay".[30] The quotation from Mainwaring also indicates that the long-boat was towed but Boteler said: "The long-boat is the largest and the strongest of all such boats as are to be hoisted into a ship". [31] John White's reference to the towing of shallops shows that for expeditions such as his shallops, specifically chosen for their qualities, were of the size necessary for their ultimate use in exploring or fishing and were not part of a ship's normal complement of boats.

Although the early references to Basque, Biscay, and French shallops have been stressed it is obvious from the various purposes for which shallops were used in the English colonies that all boats called shallops could not have been of the same form and construction. Boteler's definition of a shallop's " . . . peculiar employment . . . to row speedily upon all occasions" is not compatible with Argall's "stout shallop" to carry corn or the many shallops employed in transporting casks of tobacco. Inasmuch as the Basque or Biscay shallop seems to have been the parent from which the other variations developed it will be necessary to define it first.

Unfortunately there is no ready-made definition of a Biscay shallop and to develop a description we must turn to two related but larger craft which have been defined — the *barcaza* of Cadiz and the *barca longa* that was employed around the coasts of Portugal and Spain. In French the names of the two became *barcasse* (eventually *becasse*) and *barque longue*. Aubin's *Dictionaire de Marine*, a French work with Dutch equivalents published in Amsterdam in 1702, describes the barcaza as an undecked boat with a high stem and relatively sharp ends having a length of between 30 and 40 feet, a breadth of 8 or 9 feet, and depth of about 5 feet. Although it could be rowed with seven or more oars on each side a single square sail on a mast stepped about amidships was the usual mode of propulsion. When making a long passage it was customary to set a small square sail on a short mast stepped right in the bow. If caught in a bad storm the crew could lower the mainmast and step the smaller foremast in its place. The barcaza was considered an excellent sailer.

In the *Dictionaire du Gentilhomme* by le Sieur Guillet, published in The Hague in 1686, and in Aubin's work a *barque longue* — " . . . is small undecked vessel, longer and shallower than ordinary barques, with a sharp bow, which is propelled by sails and oars. It has the form of a shallop and in some places is called a double-shallop".

L'Architecture Navale by F. Dassie, 1677, gives the dimensions of a typical barque longue as — length from stem to stern 40 feet, breadth 9 feet, and depth 4½ feet, essentially the same as those given above by Aubin.

In the fifteenth century the Portuguese had vessels of the same general type known as barchas; the later form of the word is barca. Prince Henry the Navigator, in his efforts to discover a sea route to India, established his headquarters at Sagres in 1419 and soon after began sending a ship or two every year down the west coast of Africa but they did not pass beyond Cape Bojador a little south of the Canary Islands. This cape hardly shows as such on a modern chart; it is low and sandy, hardly visible from a distance. From October to April the cape is shrouded in fog and beaten by heavy seas — offshore at all times are treacherous currents and reefs. And in the fifteenth century there were mythical dangers beyond. All combined to turn back Prince Henry's explorers.

Under the command of one of his most skillful captains, Gil Eanes, Prince Henry sent out a barcha in 1433 with orders to pass Cape Bojador. The fears that had turned back the earlier vessels kept Gil Eanes from passing beyond the Canaries but in the same barcha the next year he did double the dreaded cape thus taking the first major step in opening the route around Africa to India. In 1894 Rear Admiral Joao Braz de Oliveira made a study of the types of vessels employed by the early Portuguese explorers and Figure 2 is based on his sketch of a barcha of 1430.[32] Although explorers in general have always been partial to small vessels it is obvious that the barcha must have been an able type.

Figure 2. Portuguese barcha, 1430. After Oliveira.

The two-masted square rig described for the barcaza and shown in the above mentioned sketch was widely portrayed by the marine artists of the Netherlands during the seventeenth and eighteenth centuries and it was employed in particular on various type of 'pinks' such as those that worked off the beach at Scheveningen. Both the mainsail and foresail were relatively deep and narrow. Originally the foresail had about one quarter of the area of the main but it grew larger with the passing of time. Because the foremast was usually located as far forward as possible, the small foresail was not normally set when beating to windward unless a bowsprit was fitted to which the tacks and bowlines could be led. Later other means were employed to support the weather leech of the foresail when beating. Figure 3 shows a small Dutch "pink" working to windward under her mainsail only.

Figure 3. Dutch 'pink'. After van de Velde.

It will be noticed that she has reef points in her mainsail — earlier boats reduced sail area by removing bonnets, panels about equal in depth to the reefs shown which were secured by lacing lines to the bottom of the main body of the sail. Through many ramifications, this basic two-masted square rig developed into the many versions of the lug rig which were so prominent along the English and French coasts.

Although some of these descriptions and the pictorial evidence may seem too late to be valid for determining the characteristics of a boat employed in the first quarter of the seventeenth century, the previously mentioned Portuguese manuscript also has a drawing of an open vessel called a barco; an outline drawing of it is reproduced in Figure 4. Compared to the batel this barco has very fine ends which would indicate a relatively fast sailer. Scaled down to a small boat, however, the barco's form might be too fine for the performance of such jobs as the recovery of anchors. We might expect a ship's shallop to be something between the barco and the batel which would still be in accordance with Garcia de Palacio's statement that a ship's chalupa was more finely modelled than its batel.

In light of the qualities of certain American small craft of the second half of the nineteenth century, it is easy to account for the existence of a superior type of small craft associated with ports on the Bay of Biscay at the beginnng of the seventeenth century. Whales had been captured by various seafaring peoples since early times, but the first systematic commercial whaling operations were undertaken by men from the Basque provinces of France and Spain, starting in the tenth century. The cities of Bayonne, Biarritz, St. Jean de Luz, and San Sebastian were important centers for these operations, which supplied all of Europe with oil and whalebone, and other towns were active. So successful was the

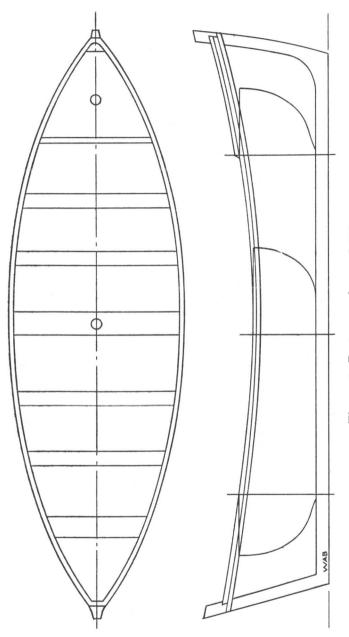

Figure 4. Portuguese barco, 1616.

pursuit of the Biscay right whale (Balaena biscayaensis) that it became almost extinct. During the fifteenth century the Basques extended their range as far as Iceland and early in the sixteenth century they established the Newfoundland fishery. Such operations required and, in the long period of time covered, developed particularly suitable small boats. In other words, the esteemed Biscay shallop was a whaleboat.

The second major phase of the whale industry followed the Spitzbergen voyage of Willem Barents in 1596 and Henry Hudson's in 1607 which discovered the Greenland whale (Balaena mysticetus). These whales showed little fear of ships and were easily captured. The Netherlands and England sent out ships and Basques were hired for a large part of each crew especially as harpooners. Presumably the Biscay shallops were also taken along — they definitely were carried on a Dutch colonizing and whaling expedition sent out to the Delaware River region in 1632 according to a report by David Pieterszoon de Vries.[33] With this whaling connection it can easily be understood how the Biscay shallop came to be known and adapted by the Dutch and English.

One unsolved shallop mystery, however, is the "halfe shallop" mentioned in two reports of Bartholomew Gosnold's exploring voyage to New England in 1602; there seem to be no others. Gabriel Archer and John Brereton each mention the hoisting out of "half of our shallop" and indicate that it was a unit capable of carrying people safely. In Archer's reference Gosnold's bark *Concord* was well off the coast of the present state of Maine when "we hoysed out halfe of our shallop, and sounding had then eightie fadome. . . ".[34] Later, when *Concord* was at anchor in what is now Provincetown harbor, Brereton reported ". . . we hoisted out the one half of our shallop and Captain Bartholomew Gosnold, myself and three others went ashore, . . . so returning towards evening to our shallop (for by that time the other part was brought ashore and set together) . . . .".[35]

Although in recent years a small dinghy of foamed plastic construction was sawed in two lengthwise and one half successfully demonstrated under sail, it is highly unlikely that the 1602 shallop of wooden construction would have been so divided. Modern sectional hunting skiffs in which transverse bulkheads at each end of the sections are bolted together to form the complete craft offer one possible solution to the problem. Small boats in sections were not unknown in Gosnold's time. An expedition to Honduras in 1596 carried — "a pinnesse in six quarters to be set together with skrewes, . . ."[36] In those days "to quarter" meant to divide into parts fewer or more than four. Thus it is possible that *Concord*'s shallop might have been cut amidships and each half fitted with a bulkhead that could be bolted to the other when the full craft was needed although a transverse bulkhead in the middle of the full shallop would have been a bit of a nuisance at times. It is possible that longitudinal strengthening pieces were added on the gunwales and keel. Whatever the actual construction may have been the carrying of the shallop in halves gave the expedition a larger shallop than the restricted stowage space on *Concord* could otherwise have allowed. The full shallop in this case could carry at least twenty-five men. When it came time for the ship to return to England no attempt was made to cut the shallop apart again — her painter was cut, and she was abandoned at sea.[37]

CHAPTER II

Colonial Development

ALTHOUGH the basic Biscay shallop was primarily a whaleboat, the type was so modified to meet the requirements of other employment in the North American colonies that whaleboats eventually became a separate class. When used for its original purpose or carried as a ship's boat, the shallop was probably completely open. Only scattered information is available concerning the actual details of the many shallops mentioned in the seventeenth-century records of Virginia and Maryland. Considering their general use for transporting casks of tobacco it is probable that most of them were open, too, with perhaps small cuddies to shelter their crews.

In Virginia a small shallop of about 1630 had a keel length of 18 feet 6 inches and a breadth of 6 feet 6 inches; for equipment she had masts, oars, a yard, and a rudder. Nails were provided by the builder — 1100 ordinary and 120 clench. Payment consisted of 120 pounds of tobacco, worth at the time about 40 shillings, plus the help of a boy and the providing of his food. As the building of this shallop was ordered by the court in the settlement of an argument, the above is hardly the true value of the shallop.[1] Another shallop of the same period, size and age not given, was purchased for 400 pounds of tobacco, the equivalent of 6 pounds 13 shillings in money.[2] The first mentioned shallop could hardly be classed as a burdensome carrier of tobacco casks. Yet a third shallop of the 1630's, built on the Eastern Shore, would have been of a more useful size. Her length, probably that of her keel, was 26 feet and she had masts, yards, and oars.[3]

As for Maryland shallops it soon became apparent to the fur traders at Kent Island that cargo needed protection and at least two of the settlement's three shallops, *Firefly* being one, were decked for half their lengths.[4] The 1641 inventory of the estate of Thomas Adams, a member of the House of Burgesses, listed a shallop with an old sail.[5] Governor Leonard Calvert's shallop had a keel length of 23 feet.[6] In 1644 a shallop with sail, rigging, and oars was judged to be worth fourteen hundred-weight of tobacco and casks.[7] The defendant in a court case in 1649 concerning repairs to a shallop stated that " . . . hee put in a false Keele uppon the Tymbers and spiked and trunnelled them and put in 2 Timbers before and 2 abaft and fitted a place for a foremast and put a Stepp therein".[8] The following from a bill of sale dated 4 December 1650 shows that, in developing from a simple whaleboat, some craft then termed shallops were large enough to require their own small boats: "Witnes my hand that I Zephania Smith of Providence (Annapolis) in Annarundell County in the Province of Mariland have sold and already delivered unto Robert Simpkin of the same place a Shallopp newly trymmed and fitted, in burthen 12 Tuns more or lesse with a small Boate belonging to her and Ropes Sailes grapling Cable and all things else wch nowe doe belong to her as they nowe are, . . .".[9]

At least one of the first two shallops at Plymouth, the one brought on *Mayflower* or that for which timber was cut during the stay at Provincetown, had some sort of a cuddy which may only have been suitable for storing food and other supplies.[10] The Plymouth colonists also recognized the need for cargo protection, for late in 1625 Bradford wrote concerning one of the shallops constructed by the unfortunate carpenter in the spring of the previous year — "They had laid a litle deck over her midships to keepe ye corne drie, but ye men were faine to stand it out all weather without shelter; . . .".[11]

In 1635 a large shallop trading with the Indians in Connecticut had the reverse arrangement — open amidships with cuddies forward and aft each large enough to hold two men. Six men formed the crew of this shallop and they were instructed to anchor in the river and not go ashore until trading was finished. Two men amidships were to conduct the trading while the other four with their guns were to be divided, two in the fore cuddy and two in the after one. These men, firing out of loop-holes in the bulkheads of the cuddies, could clear out the middle of the boat at the first sign of trouble.[12]

Other accounts from New England and particularly Boston until about 1660 are concerned mostly with the employment of shallops for trading voyages and fishing, but one reference mentions a shallop sailing from Virginia to Boston after a shipwreck.[13] At times the words boat and shallop are used interchangeably, but in many instances a boat was obviously not a shallop. Winthrop mentioned a 2-ton, a 3-ton, and a 10-ton shallop as well as a "great shallop" from Pascataquack (now Portsmouth, N.H.) which was wrecked on the rocks off Annisquam in November 1635.[14] By 1631 a fishing settlement near the mouth of the Piscataqua River had six "great shallops," five "fishing boats" with sails, anchors, and cables, and thirteen skiffs.[15]

At this point it might be well to see what can be derived from the tonnage figures given for the various shallops. As discussed in another work the number of tuns of wine that a large English ship could stow — her "burden" — was calculated by multiplying together her keel length, her maximum breadth inside the planking, and her depth from the widest point to the top of the keel and dividing the product by one hundred. In the absence of information to the contrary it can be assumed that the tonnage of small craft was reckoned in the same manner with the depth being measured to the gunwale at its lowest point. Using the proportions of the Portuguese batel the approximate dimensions of a 3-ton shallop might have been — keel length 21 feet 9 inches, breadth 6 feet 4 inches, and depth 2 feet 2 inches; her overall length would have been about 26 feet. The 12-ton Maryland shallop might have been 34 feet 9 inches long on the keel, 10 feet wide, and 3 feet 6 inches deep with an overall length of nearly 42 feet. It is obvious why a small boat was listed among her equipment.

It is obvious, however, from the previously given dimensions of the 1630 shallop in Virginia that a small shallop was wider in proportion to its length than the batel. Dassie also included the dimensions of a chaloupe in his book — length over all 29 feet 6 inches, length of keel 24 feet, breadth 6 feet 6 inches, and depth 3 feet 4 inches — much deeper relatively than the batel. Using his proportions the 3-ton shallop would have had a length overall of 24 feet 7 inches, a keel length of 20 feet, a breadth of 5 feet 5 inches, and a depth of 2 feet 9 inches. For the 12-ton shallop the dimensions work out to 39 feet overall, 31 feet 9 inches on the keel, 8 feet 7 inches wide, and 4 feet 5 inches deep.

Because the settlers in Virginia and Maryland believed that the production of tobacco was the easiest and quickest way to wealth, the building of boats and ships was relatively limited until late in the seventeenth century, hence information concerning them is scarce. On the other hand in New England, which was settled with fishing and trading in mind, there was much more seafaring activity and, inevitably, more lawsuits resulting in far more court records of all types of craft. Before examining these, however, there is good pictorial evidence that establishes the appearance of seventeenth-century fishing shallops.

In the fifth century the Celtic inhabitants of Britain were pushed westward and down into Cornwall by the invading Angles and Saxons from the east. Large numbers of the Celts crossed the Channel and populated a large part of the north-western peninsula of France, the present Brittany then known as Armorica. Through the succeeding centuries these two pockets of the Celtic race maintained communications across the Channel to such an extent that even until the middle of the sixteenth century they had practically a common language. In view of such continuing contact one can rightly expect to find many items, including boats, common to both sides of the Channel.

We can assume that the employment of the Biscay shallop was not limited to whaling and that it was used for various other types of fishing from ports in western France including those in Brittany. There is good evidence for this assumption, although with the passage of time the basic craft was modified to suit the local conditions obtaining at the various ports. In Volume 30 (1944) of *The Mariner's Mirror*, Mr. R. Morton Nance gave considerable evidence for the use of a Biscay shallop type of fishing boat in the waters of western England during the seventeenth and eighteenth centuries. From such a boat there developed the famous luggers of West Cornwall.

The first boat mentioned was that shown in the original of Figure 5 which was taken from a map of church property

Figure 5. Cornish fishing boat, 1620. After Morton Nance.

dated 1620. Such a craft was probably employed in the drift
fishery for pilchards, at that time the most important of the
fisheries off the coasts of Cornwall. As may be seen in the
sketch, this boat is rigged with two masts, each carrying a
single square sail. The mainmast is stepped practically
amidships while the shorter foremast is stepped in the very
eyes of the boat; there is a long bowsprit having considerable
steeve. The rigging is sketchily drawn and it is quite confusing, but it is not an important point here. Only one man
is shown aboard, quite properly aft in the helmsman's position. No tiller is shown but considering the absence of other
details this omission can be overlooked. The original artist
did not, however, forget the fisherman's typical high-crowned, broad-brimmed hat. As one would expect, the hull
appears to be double-ended with a well-curved stem and
a straight raking sternpost on which the rudder is hung.

The drawing of a very similar boat, Figure 6, was taken

Figure 6. Cornish fishing boat, 1694. After Morton Nance.

from another map dated seventy-four years later — 1694. There is no question about this boat's occupation as in the original drawing a similarly rigged boat was shown with a net over her port side; after her square sails had been furled the yards were hoisted part way up the masts to get them out of the way of the crew. Mr. Morton Nance wrote that: "Later custom would suggest that the masts and sails would have been lowered and stowed well out of the way to port and that, following the instructions of John, xxi, 6, the net would be out on the 'hauling board' or starboard side". A crew of three is shown in each of these two boats. In the first the helmsman, with his typical hat as in the 1620 boat, this time has under his arm a proper tiller that is shipped over the rudder head. The bowsprit is much shorter than that of the 1620 boat, has less steeve, and, instead of projecting over the gunwale, it is stepped through a hole in the sheer strake to starboard of the stem. Although the perspective of the hull is poor, the mapmaker was obviously trying to portray a double-ender with a rather full bow and a fine stern.

A print of 1739 showing St. Michael's Mount in Cornwall has several similar boats, the masts being a little taller. The nearer boats have crews of three while but one man is shown in those in the distance, probably because of delineation difficulties. On the authority of a letter written by an old fisherman who went fishing as a boy in the first quarter of the eighteenth century, Mr. Morton Nance noted that the crew of a Cornish fishing boat at that time numbered six men and a boy, the same number as traditional in Breton sardine boats.

While the foregoing discussion of Cornish fishing vessels may seem immaterial and irrelevent, it pertains directly to the fishing shallops of New England, as the town of Marblehead, Massachusetts, was settled in 1629 as a plantation of Salem by fishermen from Cornwall and the Channel Islands. While Plymouth, Salem, and Boston were settled by groups desiring freedom from the established church in England, fishing was the only reason for the establishing of Marblehead and many other communities. Within a decade its unruly inhabitants had made it the greatest town for fishing in New England and had separated from Salem.

Knowing of the traditional conservatism of fishermen around the world there can be little doubt that these Marblehead settlers constructed locally the type of boat that they had employed at home. Once the type was established on the western side of the Atlantic, this same conservatism would have retained it for a considerable period. Local conditions of use — wind and sea conditions, location of fishing grounds, and species of fish caught — plus the inevitable effects of whim and fashion were responsible for changes in the type.

Curiously enough, there is a strong possibility that the

mapmakers who drew the Cornish fishing boats with crews of three may not have been wrong. A map of the New England coast showing the region between Cape Ann and the Kennebec river that has been dated about 1680 shows two small fleets of what can only be fishing shallops. Anchored between Cape Ann and the Isle of "Sholes", riding to the prevailing south-westerly wind on a much used early fishing ground, are four boats with their masts and sails lowered and stowed in accordance with the later Cornish practice mentioned by Mr. Morton Nance. One can hardly expect, however, to be able to determine whether they are properly stowed to port! Now each of these four boats has a crew of three, all of whom are properly outfitted with the high-crowned, broad-brimmed hat such as worn by the lone helmsman in Figure 5. Unless there was a widespread artistic conspiracy which dictated that three figures were enough in any boat, the crews of three in this small fleet corroborate the evidence of the 1694 and 1739 Cornish boats.

Farther north on the map, sailing into the coast near Wood "Iland" and Cape Elizabeth, Maine, are three boats carrying two-masted square rigs like those in Figures 5 and 6. Unfortunately for our crew argument only the helmsman of each boat is shown — the others may be sleeping. But to settle the crew question, for early New England fishing shallops at least, we do not have to depend upon small sketches. In 1663 it was recorded that fishing shallops were manned by four men — the master, the midship man, the foremast man, and one man who was left ashore to dry the fish caught up by the other three.[16] Thus the unknown mapmaker who drew three men in each of his shallops off the Isles of "Sholes" was quite correct.

An interesting law case in 1662 further corroborates the crew of three. This was a suit tried in the June Quarterly

Court of Essex County, Massachusetts: "Mr. Moses Maverick & Company versus John Trumboll, master of the ship *Blossome*. Trespass. For over-running and sinking a shallop riding at anchor at sea, belonging to the plaintiff, Frances Hooper being master of the said shallop. Verdict for the plaintiff. Appealed to Court of Assistants".[17] In addition to the master of this shallop there were two others aboard — William Carter, midshipman, and Elias Fortin (or Fontewnes or Fontines), foreshipman.

This was an unusual case and it almost seems as though the crew wanted the shallop sunk. As might be expected the evidence was confused. The three members of the crew stated that their shallop was anchored about six or seven leagues off shore while they were fishing. At about nine or ten o'clock one morning they saw a ship about four leagues away heading for them—"which ship did not hail them, but ran aboard them near the midship of the boat and sunk her".[18] Hooper, the shallop's master, grabbed the ship's head structure and was taken aboard without a wetting. The other two were eventually pulled from the water. The three further testified — " . . . that the boat was of seven tons, good and strong and well conditioned and fitted for another voyage, the midshipman being shipped for another voyage as master; also that her sails and all other rigging were good and new at the beginning of the last voyage, only the roade, though put into the boat the last voyage, were not so good as the owners expected".[19]

Another fisherman, one Mighell Combs, stated that while on the fishing grounds about a month earlier he saw a ship coming in from the sea — ". . . knowing not what shee was: wee came to sayle closs Uppon a wind to speak with her: wee saw the sayd shipp strinbling in neere with Frances Hooprs. shallupp: who was at ancor and a Fishing Rann her

Full abbord & sunk her in the sea: butt might have esylie escaped the sayed shallopp if they had pleased: for they had sea Roome Inuff & the wind at thire pleasure: to go Ither a head or a starne of them; with Resonable Care: . . .".[20]

A seaman on the ship testified, however, that he heard Carter and Fortin say that the next day they had planned to return to port and haul the boat as she was old and rotten and not fit to go to sea. Carter and Fortin also said that they had veered their anchor rode which statement was corroborated by one of the ship's passengers. The latter witness stated that the ship's captain, Mr. Trumble, — " . . . desiring to speak with a shallop riding at anchor, they ran against the said shallop, sinking her".[21] The veering of the anchor rode leads one to the suspicion that as the ship was heading to pass to leeward of the anchored shallop the rode was paid out deliberately to effect the sinking of the old and rotten shallop.

The case of Maverick vs. Trumboll and other court records can be combined to provide fairly complete information as to the fittings and equipment of fishing shallops and the outfits of their crews during the second half of the seventeenth centnry. Mr. Maverick's shallop with all her furniture was appraised at 65 pounds. Appraisals of two shallops in April 1675 shows what was probably included in the valuation of his shallop.[22]

> for shallop *Edward* & *Thomas*.
>
> | | |
> |---|---:|
> | The standing and running riggin half worne | £2-10-0 |
> | A mainsaile about 90 yds. ⅔ worne | 1-10-0 |
> | A foresayle about 45 yds att 12d | 2- 5-0 |
> | 2 Cables worne | 6-10-0 |
> | 2 Anchors | 4- 0-0 |
> | 1 Iron Pott & Pott hooke | 0- 8-0 |
> | The vesell, and masts & yards, & a boate | 40- 0-0 |

A Compass & Pump & other small trifles	0-10-0
The whole Amo unto	£57-13-0

The Penobscot Shallop thatt Roads went out in

2 Peeces of cable	£2-0-0
1 Anchor, and a broken Anchor	3-0-0
A mainsail & foresaile old & a Bonnett	2-0-0
Standing & running riggin very old	1-0-0
One Iron Pott & a kettle & a compass	1-0-0
The Hull, masts & Canoe	6-0-0
This Boat Amo unto	£15-0-0

The Penobscot Shallop — whether *Penobscot* was her name or merely an indication of her home waters is unknown — was obviously an old boat in poor condition and she was very likely smaller than *Edward* & *Thomas* as she had a canoe rather than a boat. The relative sizes of the sails in *Edward* & *Thomas* agree with those of the basic two-masted square rig on the Cornish boats. The mention of the bonnet in the inventory of the Penobscot Shallop shows that she at least did not have reef points in her sails. The relatively high values of the anchors and cables are interesting.

Details of the arrangement of the hull of such a shallop may be derived from an agreement between Erasmus James, a boatbuilder of Marblehead, and three fishermen of the same town to repair a shallop that evidently had been damaged by fire. James was to rebuild the shallop: ". . . one whole strake higher than her first build, to pull out what planks were necessary, either under or above water, and put in new, to seal it, make up the rooms and do all other ax work within board and without fitting for the sea, excepting anchor stocks, oars, masts, yards, tiller and chimney. He was to find all plank, timber, oakum, tar, boards, speeches, nails, and to finish the work as soon as possible, 'god sending him life helth & conveniant weather to work in'. He was not to take any other piece of work to hinder him from doing this, except for a day or two at a time, and was to be paid 17 pounds sterling in the spring of 1670 at a convenient stage at Marblehead, in dry and refuse cod fish, before June 25."[23]

From this we can deduce that fishing shallops were sheathed on the inside. This shallop at least was partially decked in order to provide a cuddy for the crew which was fitted with a fireplace that required a chimney. The rooms mentioned were open spaces extending nearly across the vessel between transverse bulkheads in which the men stood while fishing; presumably the shallop was decked over the fish holds between the rooms. While waves could and did slop aboard into these standing rooms, the bulkheads restricted the flow of water fore and aft so that the vessel could not fill and founder. In later times, possibly even then, it was the practice to fit covers on the standing rooms when the men were not fishing. On 17 June 1675 one George Maning deposed that when the trading shallop *Philipp* was riding at anchor off Mount "de Zart" she was boarded by pirates who "opened the hatches & tooke all my peltery".[24] This indicates either that her rooms had covers or that she had a full deck with normal hatches over a long hold.

For the miscellaneous gear aboard a fishing shallop and the outfits of the crew members we return to Mr. Maverick's vessel. The following items belonging to the shallop were lost when she was run down and sunk by the ship *Blossome*: "One Nett, 3 li. [pounds]; 1 Rope belonging to ye nett, 10 s[hillings]; 1 old nett, 40 s. & 1 Rope, 10s; ½Barrell of oyle, 1 li.; 3 C. ¾ [hundredweight] of good Codd fish, 7 li.; 2 B. of Salte, 6 s. & Bagg, 5 s.; a splitting knife 2s. 6d. [pence];

and Iron pott, 5 s. 6 d.; total 14 li. 19s." The master of the shallop, Frances Hooper, lost "A Cap, 13s.; a Coate, 10s; a Coate of Tho. Roses, 10s. [probably the shore man]; 1 pr. of Briches, 10s.; 1 pr. of drawes, 3s.; 1 pr. of shooes, 3s.; 1 pr. of stokings, 2s.; a thoust [?], 2s., gloves & mittings, 3s; 1 li. of candles, 6d; hookes & lines, 1 li.; a gimblett, 3d.; a kniufe, 6d.; a steele, 3d.; total 3 li. 17s. 6d.". The following goods belonging to William Carter, the midshipman, were aboard: "A weascote, 12s.; 1 pr. of shooes, 6s.; 1 pr. of shooes more, 2s.; 2 pr. of stockings, 4s.; 1 pr. of Briches, 4s.; 1 pr. of mittings, 1s. 6d.; 1 kniufe, 1s; hookes & lines, 1 li.; total 2 li. 16s.". Elias Fortin's gear included: 1 pr. of Bootes, 1 li.; a long Cape, 1 li.; a sute of ledr. stuf, 10s.; a Coate & brichis, 10s.; a Capp, 4 s.; 1 pr. of stockings, 2 s.; hookes & lines, 1 li.; total, 4 li. 6s.".[25] It is interesting to note that while the nets were considered part of the shallop's equipment, each of the men had his own hooks and lines.

While we can describe the arrangement, fittings, and rig of a New England fishing shallop with fair certainty, such details are lacking for the Chesapeake Bay shallops and in neither case do we have any really sound information concerning form. Considering the geography of the Iberian Peninsula and the French and Spanish influence on the Netherlands, it is not surprising that the ship's boat of the middle seventeenth century shown in Figure 7, catalogued as a "chaloupe" from the Netherlands,[26] exhibits many of the characteristics of the Portuguese batel, Figure 1. In English units her length is about 26 feet overall, her breadth to the outside of the planking 8 feet 4 inches, and her depth 3 feet 3 inches; relatively she is a much beamier craft than any of those for which dimensions have been given. Similarly shaped hulls may still be found in the Netherlands and adjacent countries.

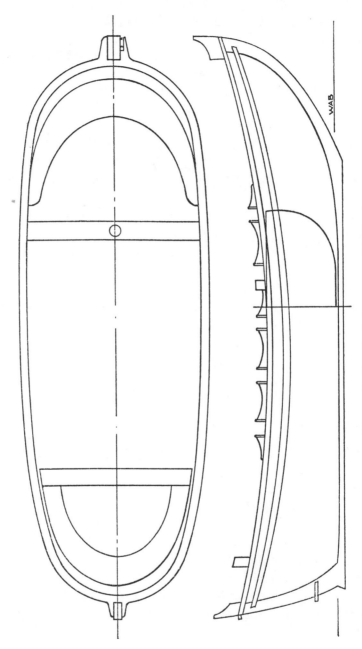

Figure 7. Dutch chaloupe, ca. 1650.

The position of the single mast in this chaloupe indicates that she probably carried two fore-and-aft sails; her
mainsail was undoubtedly a spritsail. Stout vertical timbers
on which to hang leeboards are fitted port and starboard a
little abaft the mast thwart. She has a sheave on the starboard side of her stern but there are no provisions for the in-
stallation of a windlass.

Also from the Netherlands is the Egmonder "Zee-Pinck,"
Figure 8, taken from Witsen's great work of 1671.[27] As the

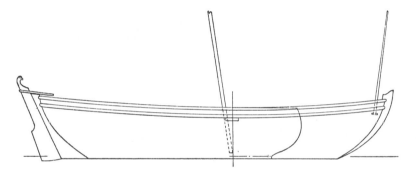

Figure 8. Egmonder pinck. After Witsen.

Netherlands lacked suitable harbors, such craft were designed
to work off the North Sea beaches. She has no external keel—
her bottom is perfectly flat and is extra thick. The dimensions of this pink in English units are about 32 feet 6 inches
in length overall, 11 feet 2 inches in breadth, and 4 feet 2
inches in depth. For a considerable period Egmonder pinks
were the largest Dutch fishing vessels and were an old type
even in Witsen's time.

A rigged pink of about 1620 on the beach, based on a
painting by H. C. Vroom, is shown in Figure 9.[28] Although a
beach boat, she has many of the features that we have noted
in connection with New England fishing shallops which, of

Figure 9. A pink on the beach. After Vroom.

course, were harbor-based craft. Her rig is obvious and needs little comment. With no bowsprit her foresail could not have been carried when beating to windward. Her mainsail is fitted with bowlines and it has a bonnet instead of the reef points shown in Figure 3.

This pink's main mast appears to be supported by a heavy thwart forward of which she is decked; a low open rail extends from the stem aft to the mast thwart. There is a short length of deck at the stern — about midway between this and the mast thwart is another short section forming two fishing rooms. Her ends, and those of smaller craft by other artists, do not seem to be as full as those of Figures 1 and 7. Leeboards such as shown were commonly fitted even on ship's boats until about 1700; they were easily removed when not required. No evidence for their use on New England or Chesapeake shallops has yet been found. These shallops undoubtedly were built with external keels which certainly helped in sailing to windward.

Figure 10 gives the lines and rig of a late eighteenth-century Breton fishing boat from Douarnenez.[29] The relationship with the batel and the pink is obvious and demonstrates how slowly changes were made.

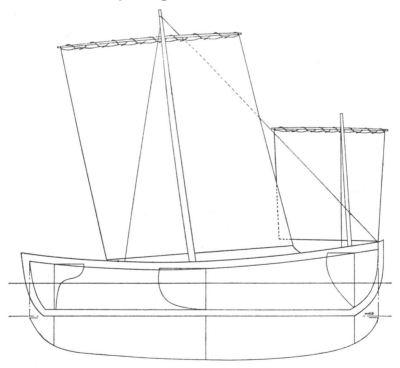

Figure 10. Douarnenez fishing boat, end of 18th century. After Paris.

❀❀❀❀❀❀❀❀❀❀❀❀❀❀❀❀❀❀❀❀❀❀❀❀❀❀❀❀❀❀❀❀

CHAPTER III

Early Sloops

A SURE WAY to stir up a friendly argument at any yacht club is to ask the difference between a cutter and a sloop. During the ensuing discussion quote the following:

"Sloops — Are Sail'd & Masted as Mens fancys leads them sometimes wth One Mast, wth Two, and wth Three, wth Burmudoes, Shoulder of Mutton, Square Lug & Smack Sails, they are in Figure either Square or Round Stern'd".

So wrote Thomas Riley Blanckley in his manuscript nautical dictionary of 1732 titled *A Naval Expositor*; this work appeared in printed form in 1750. About one hundred years earlier — 1629 to be exact — this derivative of the Dutch word that is most familiar to us today first appeared in the written English language. This was in a letter dated 22 January 1629 from English merchants in charge of a trading station at Armagon on the east coast of India to the superiors at Bantam on Java. They requested that a small vessel be furnished to them in order that they might conduct trading operations with nearby ports in the manner of the Dutch who kept — " . . . always some 5 or 6 sloopes and junks trading . . . from porte to porte".[1] In the years following this introduction the term sloop meant many things as Blanckley's definition suggested.

Some thirty years after this first appearance of sloop we start to find in the British records some confusion between sloops and shallops. In the list compiled by Samuel Pepys of vessels in the Royal Navy of England from May 1660 to 25 March 1686 there are the names, dimensions, number of men, and number of guns for twenty-two sloops. No shallops are listed although the same information is given for several small smacks with crews of only two.[2] The records, however, still included a number of references to shallops.

On 12 March 1662 Lord Windsor asked for two double shallops for Jamaica; about a month later the Admiralty estimated that two 40 foot shallops would cost £120.[3] On 14 November 1666 — "for the defence of the Island (Isle of Wight) ordered that a shallop with a master and two mariners . . . be employed at Bembridge, . . .". The estimate for this shallop submitted on 8 February 1667 gave the following details — " . . . to be in length 40 ft., 9 ft. breadth, 3½ ft. deep. Masts, yards, sails, rigging, a grapnel and rope and ten oars".[4] The smallest of the sloops in Pepys's list, *Dove* built in 1672, had a keel length of 40 feet, a breadth of 9 feet 10 inches, and a depth of 4 feet.

The following item bears the date of 10 June 1668 — "To prevent the export of wool chiefly from Romney Marsh, which export was prejudicial to the manufacture of clothing in England, a request was made for two small vessels, one to lie betwixt Rye and Dover, the other to ply upon the coast of France where the boats and shallops usually resort". On 2 September 1669 — "Ordered that two double shallops lie off the Kentish coast." — but by 2 December 1670 — "HM. having noticed how ineffectual in preventing wool smuggling they are, the two sloops on the Kentish coast are to be paid off".[5] About three years later and undoubtedly not pertaining to the same vessels — similar patrolling vessels had been stationed off West County ports — there are orders dated 8 and 20 October 1673 for the paying off of the *Hawk* shallop and the *Fox* shallop.[6] The latter may have been the same *Fox* that on 27 February 1674 was ordered restored to — " . . . Mr. Curtis who bought her 'in joynts from Zeland' and fitted her out a year since in attendance on Prince Rupert".[7]

The oldest of the sloops on Pepys's list was *Dunkirk* captured from the port of that name in 1656. Of 33 tons burden, she measured 40 feet on the keel, had a breadth of 12 feet 6 inches, and her depth was 4 feet 6 inches; her crew in home waters in time of war was 20 men and she carried two guns. In connection with this sloop, the following interesting bits pertain to captured privateers from Dunkirk and Ostend that had been brought into English ports. Listed as sloops at Dover in August 1676 were *Petit Louis*, burden 50 tons, with two guns and a crew of twenty two, and *Petit La Force*, "a little open vessel of 6 tons in burden, formerly a Greenland shallop, carrying 11 men".[8] In the Downs in September 1676 were *Ann* of Ostend, "a square-sterned open sloop, with 2 guns and 20 men", and *St. Teresa* of Dunkirk, "a square-sterned sloop with a deck, a small head and a figure of a cat thereon, her foresail and foretopsail furling aloft, 38 men, 3 guns, and 1 pederero".[9]

A contract dated March 1691 began with a reference to a substantial sloop for rowing and sailing and ended with an item concerning the delivery of the shallop to His Majesty's Yard at Deptford. This craft — sloop or shallop — was 45 feet long overall, 10½ feet in breadth, and 5 feet deep. She had a decked-over forepeak 9 feet long and a 7 foot long stateroom aft that was fitted with a platform, seats, and arms chests. Between the forepeak and the stateroom she had fixed thwarts spaced 5 feet apart under each of which was a tight transverse bulkhead so that the spaces between the fixed thwarts were like the wells in a fishing boat. Loose thwarts were arranged between the fixed ones. She had two masts arranged to lower but there was no mention in the contract of other spars or her sails.[10]

Some details of a shallop employed as a collier can be gleaned from a bill dated 1692 for the lengthening of *Henry & John*. Her dimensions before and after were not given but her capacity was increased by 33 chalders, equivalent to about 15 tons burden. She had a cabin and her equipment included a capstan, two pumps, and a compass. Before lengthening her sails included at least a square sail under the bowsprit, courses on fore and main masts, and some sort of a mizzen; she may also have carried a main topsail. During the period she was in the yard she received the following new spars; bowsprit, fore mast, fore topmast, fore topsail yard, main topmast, and main yard. Among the old items to be sold after completion of the work was a mizzen, so *Henry & John* may not have carried one after conversion.[11]

Some of the confusion between shallops and sloops can be clarified if we assume that the naval shallops were undecked craft propelled by oars and sails, hence in the expendable boat category that would not have been listed. Although we have previously noted that both Guillet in 1686 and Aubin in 1702 stated that an open barque longue was sometimes called a double shallop the latter designation was more commonly applied to a decked version of the type. Considering the references to the privateer sloops from Dunkirk and Ostend, that the oldest of the sloops in Pepys's list came from Dunkirk, and the problems that might have arisen in case of the inadvertent omission of the adjective "double" we can understand the gradual shift in designation from "double shallop" to "sloop." Following are the particulars of some of the sloops from Pepys's list:

Name	Date	Keel Length	Breadth	Depth	Burden	L/B	D/B	Crew*	Guns
Dunkirk	1656	40'-0"	12'-6"	4'-6"	33	3.20	0.360	20	2
Bonetta	1673	61'-0"	13'-0"	5'-0"	57	4.69	0.384	10	4
Dove	1672	40'-0"	9'-10"	4'-0"	19	4.07	0.407	10	4
Fanfan	1665	44'-0"	12'-0"	5'-8"	33	3.67	0.473	30	4
Spye	1666	44'-0"	11'-0"	4'-0"	28	4.00	0.364	10	4
Emsworth	1667	40'-0"	13'-7"	4'-9"	39	2.95	0.350	10	4
Whipster	1672	58'-0"	14'-6"	5'-0"	64	4.00	0.345	10	4

*Crew in home waters in time of war.

As previously noted *Dunkirk* was the oldest of the listed sloops and *Dove* the smallest. *Bonetta* was one of the largest; her sister *Woolwich* was lost in a hurricane at Barbadoes. By 1683 all except *Bonetta* and *Fanfan*, sometimes classed as a sixth-rate, had been lost at sea, cast away, captured, or sold as useless. *Fanfan* and *Spye* were built in Harwich Dockyard " . . . of small Draught of Water, to clear the sands before this Harbour, then much infested with Dutch Picaroons". *Fanfan*, and presumably *Spye* too, had oars for propulsion in calms and when first put in service carried but two guns.[12]

But what was the rig of these Pepysian sloops? What rigs would be a better question as there were at least three that might have been carried and it is improbable that all were rigged alike. *Fanfan, Emsworth*, and *Spye* had three-masted rigs with topmasts on all three masts. They all carried the square spritsail forward, courses and topsails on their fore and main masts, and a mizzen, probably a lateen sail; *Fanfan* had a square mizzen topsail as well.[13] *Bonetta*, as shown in a drawing from 1678 by Willem Van de Velde the Younger, was a square-sterned vessel with only two masts; she had a very tall flagstaff aft. Her complete rig is not shown but the three deadeyes shown on her starboard

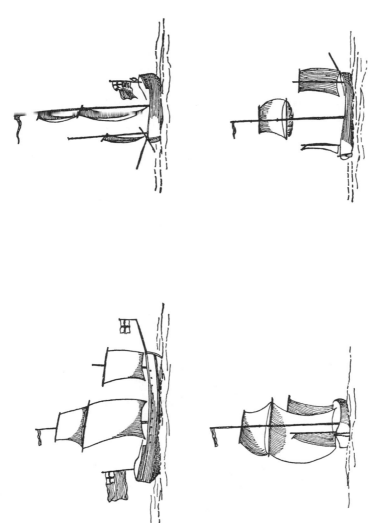

Figure 11. Sloops of the Royal Navy, 1660-1680. After van de Velde.

main channel, a sail allowance list, and other sketches com-
bine to indicate that she carried something like the basic Biscay shallop rig — a small square foresail, a much larger main,
a main topsail that may have been set flying, and probably
a spritsail forward. Other Van de Velde sketches from 1673
seem to show similarly rigged round-sterned sloops with
short-gaff mizzens set on their flagstaffs. These rig variations are shown in Figure 11.

The third possible rig is indicated by the description of
the privateer *St. Teresa* of Dunkirk, which had a foresail and
fore topsail that were furled aloft, and the fact that *Whipster*,
is further described under the sloop classification as a brigantine. No other vessel in Pepys's entire list is so designated.
Some brigantines built for the British navy between 1691
and 1695 had two masted square rigs similar to that shown
in Figure 12. The construction and rigging of the fore mast
was that of the contemporary ship. There was a lower mast

Figure 12. Brigantine, late 17th century.

and a fidded topmast complete with a platform top and all the associated standing rigging. The fore course and fore top-sail were of normal ship proportions and were furled aloft on their yards. The main mast shown is a single pole but some of these brigantines had separate main topmasts. The main course — deep and narrow in shape — was furled by lowering the yard to the deck; a light main topsail was set flying. These brigantines also carried a spritsail forward, a main staysail, a jib set flying, and other "small sails".

The brigantine was another confusing type in the seventeenth century and was usually described as a small light vessel propelled by oars and sails designed for fighting or giving chase. One of the brigantines whose rig was essentially that described above was *Dispatch* built in 1692.[14] Her keel length was 52 feet 6 inches, her breadth 16 feet 7 inches, and her depth 6 feet 2½ inches; her burden was 77 tons. She was armed with six small carriage guns and two swivels. Although shorter than *Whipster* she was wider and deeper and to provide suffcent power for propulsion by oars her crew numbered 35. Thus we can see that there was nothing in *Whipster*'s dimensions, proportions, number of guns, or size of crew to indicate any great difference from the other sloops; hence it is possible that rig determined her designation as a brigantine.

There is one more possible rig for some of the Pepysian sloops that cannot lightly be dismissed. This is the two-masted fore-and-aft rig with at least one triangular headsail that today is known as the schooner rig. There exists a mezzotint after an undated painting by William Van de Velde, presumably the Younger who died in 1707, showing two vessels so rigged flying English colors. One is a substantial decked vessel with five ports in her bulwarks for carriage guns while the other is much smaller and open, Figure 13.

Figure 13. English vessels before 1707. After van de Velde.

None of the known yachts of the period were so rigged — yachts will be discussed later — and there is no known English term of the period for such a rig. To the French "brigantin" was the name of the light vessel for fighting or giving chase while "brigantine" was the name given to the fore-and-aft sail often fitted on such a craft. Is this a possible explanation of *Whipster* brigantine?

Turning now to North American records, William Bradford, whose journal covered the activities of the Plymouth Colony from 1620 to 1646, never mentioned sloops; he referred to small craft either as shallops or just boats. John Winthrop in writing of the events in and around Boston between 1630 to 1649 used the term sloop but three times and, as in the 1629 case, always in connection with the Dutch. On 10 December 1635 he wrote that the Dutch from New Amsterdam had sent a sloop to take possession of the mouth of the

Connecticut River but that the men already there from Massachusetts would not let the sloop's crew land.[15] A sloop from New Amsterdam went to the Thames River region in eastern Connecticut in May 1637 to try to redeem two English maids held by the Pequots — the Dutch eventually succeeded in their mission.[16] The third reference recorded the arrival of a Dutch sloop in Boston on 22 July 1643 with letters in Latin from the authorities at New Amsterdam.[17] It is obvious from such references that Winthrop recognized a definite type of small craft employed by the Dutch but not at that time by the English in New England.

In Massachusets the term sloop appeared in the court records of Suffolk County under the date of 31 January 1651/52 in an indenture relating to vessels passing through a certain bridge and loading or unloading at certain wharves — " . . . all Boates shallops Pinnases Barkes shippes Sloopes and Vessels whatsoever. . .".[18] This indicates that eight and one-half years after the Dutch sloop had brought letters to Boston enough sloops were employed in Boston waters to warrant listing the type separately and not relegating it to the general classification "Vessells". It was until November 1669 that a case involving a sloop was tried in the Essex County court; it was concerned with the breaking up of an old hulk.[19]

For the colonies south of New England there are no journals comparable to those of Bradford and Winthrop; hence court records, official minutes and reports, and occasional letters are the sources of bits and pieces of information. A sloop was first mentioned in Maryland records on 20 June 1648 — she was employed for a trading voyage up to "Wicocomco".[20] A reference in 1654 indicates that in that year sloops were generally considered to be undecked. One Edward Brisley who had been on a long voyage in a sloop sold

her to a Mr. Preston, who, Brisley stated — ". . . Should have
the Sloope with all his heart, for She was an Ugly Bitch, . . .
for he was resolved to goe noe More in Such open Vessells . . .".[21] Perhaps the earliest record in Virginia was a
1652 contract for the building of a sloop.[22]

When we come to consider the maritime affairs of the
Dutch and Swedish colonies we are faced with problems of
translation; hence the English versions of the various reports
and letters must be viewed with caution. The 1644 report
of Governor Johan Printz of New Sweden on the lower Delaware to the Noble West India Company in Old Sweden has
several references to the colony's boats and sloops and to
English sloops.[23] This is probably the simplest translation
of the Swedish slup; there is no way of knowing, however,
whether the English would have called their vessels sloops or
shallops. The above 1648 date for the first recorded use of a
sloop in Maryland does not preclude the use of the term by
seafarers at an earlier date. Of two reports by Governor
Johan Classon Rising in 1655 the earlier mentions a sloop
and the other a shallop so the Swedes may have recognized
a difference.[24] The sloop became leaky and had been drawn
up on the land because of the lack of timber for repairs, but
it seemed as though the shallop had been in recent use.

For the Dutch settlements, however, there is little doubt
that, of the two basic types of small vessels mentioned, sloep
became sloop in English and jaght became yacht. But now
we are faced with the problem of determining what a sloep
was in the Netherlands in the early seventeenth century. A
Dutch-Latin dictionary published in Antwerp in 1599 gave
under *sloepe* and *sloepken* — a little ship, skiff, or boat. Of
all the types of small craft that come to mind in connection
with the Netherlands only one has consistently been called a
sloep. The word was applied originally, as it still is, to an open

boat and particularly to a ship's boat, as in *reddingsloep* —
a life-boat; this is never called a *reddingboot*. Two other
meanings of sloep are now recognized. One designates a type
of fishing boat imported from France in the nineteenth century and employed until about 1930. The other refers to the
modern pleasure craft for cruising and racing that carry a
single-masted rig with two fore-and-aft sails which in America
would be called a jib and mainsail.[25] Most Dutch craft bearing this jib and mainsail rig have been and are known by
names derived from their form, constructional features, use,
or place of building — almost every possible name but sloep.

From the available accounts it appears that the small
craft employed by the Dutch around New Amsterdam whose
type name was translated into English as sloop were definitely in the open boat category propelled by both oars and
sails. There is a reference to the carriage of cattle in sloops
and boats in 1626 and as late as 1663 an open sloop was employed for a trip to Connecticut — "When the ebb was passed
we weighed anchor, passed Hellegat at low water, and arrived, by tacking and rowing, near Minnewits Island, where
we stopped".[26] There is abundant pictorial evidence for the
use of the fore-and-aft rig on small craft employed on the inland water of the Netherlands. Considering the similar rivers
and bays around New Amsterdam, it is tempting to say that
all the sloops there were fore-and-aft rigged and that this
was the difference between a sloop and a shallop. Yet in
paintings by the Van de Veldes and the others where a fleet
is depicted at sea and shore-based boats would not be present,
many of the ship's boats-sloops- had one- and two-masted
square rigs.

There is even a reference in the Dutch records to the
Plymouth colony. This is a letter written about 1628 by
Isaack de Rasieres, the chief trading agent in New Amster-

dam for the Dutch West India Company, to Samuel Blom-
maert, a merchant in Amsterdam. De Rasieres referred to
the craft employed for fishing out of Plymouth and to those
which transported corn to the Kennebec as sloops, which
would have been the proper Dutch designation as they were
undecked. He called the decked vessel that operated from the
trading post at Aptucxet at the head of Buzzards Bay a shallop, but to Bradford she was a "pinass" or "barke".[27]

The somewhat larger decked craft employed out of New
Amsterdam for local trading were classed as yachts and, as
they had considerable influence on later developments, some
discussion of them is in order. According to the above mentioned Dutch-Latin dictionary a yacht was a swift, light-built
vessel of war, commerce, or pleasure. Van Konijnenburg
noted that the yacht developed in North Holland. In contrast to the wide, bluff-bowed, flat-bottomed types usually
associated with the Netherlands, the yacht had a narrow bottom and sharper ends; hence its reputation for speed.[28] As
the type name yacht was based on form rather than rig, yachts
were of various sizes and were employed for many purposes.
They could and did carry all sorts of rigs ranging from the
normal seventeenth-century three-masted ship rig with two
square-rigged masts, a lateen on the mizzen, and a spritsail
under the bowsprit down to the single fore-and-aft sail that
Americans employed on catboats.

Henry Hudson's *Half Moon* of about 80 tons was considered a yacht and she had the normal ship rig of the period;
she measured about 63 feet from stem to sternpost with a
breadth of 18 feet. A much larger ship-rigged "advijs-yacht"
or despatch vessel of about 1670 had a length of 115 feet and
a breadth of 27 feet 5½ inches. Adriaen Block's yacht
Onrust built on Manhattan after his ship *Tiger* burned acci-
dentally in 1614 and was 44½ feet long from stem to stern

and 11½ feet wide. The State yachts employed to regulate shipping, collect revenue, prevent smuggling, and similar duties, and the Admiralty yacht, which performed various duties for the naval fleets, varied in size, but some are known to have been about 70 feet in length. The common representations of these yacht show single-masted fore-and-aft rigs. The mainsail was either a spritsail or was supported by a long gaff — both forms were boomless in the early days, there were one or two triangular sails on stays forward, and occasionally there was a square topsail. Similar yachts were also employed for commercial purposes and pleasure sailing. They also served for royal entertainment in England where the term yacht, which meant a certain form to the Dutch, was used to designate any craft used for pleasure. Figure 14

Figure 14. Dutch State yacht, second half of 17th century. After Allard.

shows a typical State yacht of the late part of the seventeenth century.

For pleasure sailing in the seventeenth century the Dutch also had the *speeljaght* — literally play yacht. While there were single-masted versions it was usually depicted with a two-masted fore-and-aft rig in which the foremast was the shorter; this was stepped well forward and the mainmast was stepped about amidships, Figure 15. Each mast carried

Figure 15. Speeljaght, early 17th century. After Rool.

a loose-footed sail that was supported by a short gaff, the English shoulder-of-mutton sail. A boom was normally fitted for the mainsail and occasionally one is shown for the foresail, too. The early seventeenth-century *speeljaght* had no head-sail, but there is sufficient evidence to indicate the existence of the two-masted fore-and-aft rig with a triangular headsail by about 1650. Another form of the two-masted fore-and-aft rig, which may not have been employed on *speeljaghts* but which was used on open boats, had jib-headed sails laced to well-raked masts, Figure 16. It seems probable that the

Figure 16. Dutch sloop, 1629. After Chatterton.

majority of the New Amsterdam yachts had fore-and-aft rigs. The earliest known view of New York, the Hartgers view, which depicted the settlement about 1626-1628 although it was not issued until 1651, shows a two-masted fore-and-aft rigged vessel without a headsail, Figure 17, that could be either a sloop or a yacht.

A watercolor in the Royal Archives in The Hague depicting New Amsterdam in 1650-3 shows one ship, six small vessels, and three Indian canoes. One of the small vessels has no mast while three have one mast with no rigging details

Figure 17. Sloop or yacht, New Amsterdam.

shown. The fifth is a single-masted fore-and-aft rigged vessel with a bowsprit and leeboards; she is carrying a triangular foresail set to the stem head and a long-gaff boomless mainsail. The sixth has a two-masted fore-and-aft rig with her masts positioned as in the *speeljaghts* and she also has a bowsprit and leeboards. She may be a trading yacht or perhaps a pleasure boat belonging to the West India Company, one of which de Vries sent out to his ship in 1653 after his ship's boat was swamped in a thunderstorm and driven out to sea.

There are various references to indicate that the New Amsterdam yachts were not very large although definite figures are lacking. Nicolaes van Wassenaer noted in 1626 that trading in the Delaware region was carried on only with yachts in order to avoid expense.[29] DeVries got into difficulties in 1633 with Governor Wouter van Twiller who did not want him to send his yacht trading to the north. Van Twiller sent alongside the yacht — " . . . a *schapan* — a flat lighter-boat, in which the whole yacht could easily have been contained — and wanted to unload the yacht, in which were five or six lasts (10 to 12 tons) of brick ballast".[30] This yacht had apparently crossed the Atlantic in company with a large ship.

In 1679 Jaspar Dankers mentioned a channel in the lower part of the bay that was — " . . . only deep enough for boats, yachts, and other small craft".[31] Early in 1680 he and his companion, Peter Sluyter, sailed up the Hudson in a yacht with about twenty passengers and "some tons of oysters aboard" that was — " . . . not so large as a common ferry boat in Holland".[32] On 19 June 1680 they sailed for Boston in a yacht which had a crew of three men and a boy besides the captain. Embarking at noon — "The wind being ahead (north-west), we tacked and towed, until we anchored at Hellgate, almost at flood tide, at four o'clock in the afternoon".[33] The rig of this yacht is open to some question. Further to the eastward, when in danger of running aground, sail had to be taken off quickly and the anchor dropped: — " . . . the anchor would not hold. We found that the spritsail had caught in the anchor stock in consequence of the hurry in lowering the sail and throwing anchor. . . ".[34] The yacht arrived in Boston at four o'clock in the afternoon of 23 June and sailed right up to the captain's house in the Milk-ditch.

✿✿✿✿✿✿✿✿✿✿✿✿✿✿✿✿✿✿✿✿✿✿✿✿✿✿✿✿✿✿✿✿✿

CHAPTER IV

A Confusion Of Sloops

O F JOHN WINTHROP'S three references to Dutch
sloops, the vessel in one case, that of the rescue of the
three English maids from the Pequots, was called a yacht by
Captain Daniel Patrick who had seen her.[1] Considering the
circumstances of the other references, it seems likely that
Winthrop's sloop meant yacht in those cases, too. One of them
was an attempted landing by the Dutch at Saybrook at the
mouth of the Connecticut in winter and in, to say the least,
an unfriendly atmosphere, while the other involved a passage
around Cape Cod in July, a journey which, as we have noted,
required four days in a yacht in 1680. Just why Winthrop
chose sloop, which meant an open rowing and sailing boat,
to apply to a decked vessel may never be known unless, being
aware that a yacht might have been of any size with any sort
of rig, he wanted to indicate a small vessel. Rig alone was
probably not the reason for, as pointed out in "Notes on a
Shallop," here is sufficient evidence to suggest that the shallop brought on *Mayflower* in 1620 had a single-masted fore-
and-aft-rig. This, however, was nine years before the term
sloop appeared in the written English language. It might
be well to point out again here that the sail known today in

America as the jib in the standard two-sail fore-and-aft rig —
the jib-and-mainsail rig — was originally and still is by the
English called the foresail.

Although de Vries referred in 1635 to his use of "one
of the Company's pleasure boats,"[2] by which he may have
meant a two-masted *speeljaght*, it is probable that the normal
yacht employed for trading and duties such as those mentioned by Winthrop was a small single-masted "State" yacht.
Apart from the details of rig previously noted one feature of
such yacht was a prominent cabin at the stern. Although some
of the yachts of New Amsterdam sailed across the Atlantic, others were built in the colony and one would not expect
such vessels to be as elaborately decorated as those constructed in the Netherlands. Although there is little on which
to base such an assumption, Figures 18 and 19 show typical
vessels of the colony after it had become New York in September 1664.

Figure 18 is from the Duke's Plan of New Amsterdam[3]
which was drawn in 1664 but showed the arrangement of the

Figure 18. Yacht, New Amsterdam, 1661. After the Duke's Plan.

town as it appeared in 1661 although all the vessels in the surrounding waters are flying the English flag. This vessel is typical of the 13 large and small single-masted vessels shown; we can safely call them yachts. Also included are six ships and a ketch. While the sketches are small, without much detail, and in all probability stylized to a certain extent, the yachts do have some definite features. The stern cabins are very prominent while the bows have no decorations. Their masts are stepped well forward, their bowsprits have considerable steeve, and they seem to have but one headsail. All the booms are long but as none of the yachts has its mainsail set we can only surmise that the gaffs were short; the long gaff sail did not acquire a boom until considerably later.

Figure 19. New York yacht, 1679. After Dankers.

The yacht in Figure 19 was presumably sketched on the spot by Jaspar Dankers in 1679; she too has the plain bow and high stern. The short-gaff mainsail is well shown and she can carry a jib in addition to her foresail. The use of the long gaff has already been mentioned and there is evidence that sprit mainsails were also employed.

In the Chesapeake region articles of agreement dated 6 May 1665 definitely calls a sloop a single-masted vessel having a fore-and-aft mainsail with a boom.[4] There may be earlier indications. In 1665 James Ffookes, a shipwright working in Accomac County on Virginia's eastern shore, agreed with Mrs. Anne Hack to build a sloop capable of carrying 35 hogsheads of tobacco. Mrs. Hack was to furnish the necessary nails and spikes and was to arrange for the cutting and shaping of the mast and boom. The description of this sloop indicates that she had some sort of a cabin forward but otherwise was open. This would agree with Brisley's comment about "Such open Vessells" and would suit her general employment of transporting casks of tobacco around Chesapeake Bay.

An early Massachusetts record of the single-masted rig on a sloop is a bill of sale dated 2 July 1685 for — " . . . one quarter part of the Sloop Called the *Amity* Burthen thirty three Tunns or thereabouts Together with one quarter part of the mast Boome, Bow Spreit, Cables Anchors Sailes, ropes rigging Boate, Oares, Tackling furniture, apparell, and all other the Materialls. . . ". This one quarter part was worth £30-2-0.[5] For comparison the bill of sale for a shallop in 1679 reads — " . . . and also three quarter parts of the good Shallop named the *Prosperus*, together with three Quarter parts of all Masts Sailes Saileyards Cables Anchors ropes Rigging Boat Oares . . .".[6]

In North America as in England there was with the

passing of time a certain amount of confusion between shallops and sloops. In a Massachusetts case tried in the Essex
County Court in November 1670, one witness referred to a
vessel as a shallop while the next witness called her a small
sloop.⁷ In the first Essex County case involving a sloop, in
November 1699, Thomas Clengen, who served in her, stated
— ". . . she was of twenty-five tons, sheathed with new plank,
her deck was new, her mainsail as good as new, not half worn,
shrouds new and all running rigging as good as new, one
cable and two dozen blocks new". This deponent further
mentioned that — "He unrigged the vessel and delivered it . . .
except one anchor, one cable and the foresail".⁸ For a vessel
with only a foresail and a mainsail it is easier to explain the
presence of two dozen blocks if we assume that she had the
two-masted square rig of a shallop rather than a jib-and-
mainsail rig. Further confusion is found in a 1671 case in
the Suffolk County Court — a "Deck Shallop or barque" was
also called a sloop by one of her crew.⁹

The presence of a "main Sheet" in company with the pre-
sent-day definition are the only indications that a small sloop
of 1727 had a single-masted rig. While her crew was ashore
she had become frozen in the ice and wind and tide had carried her to sea. Picked up and taken into Newport, Rhode
Island, an inventory of all the items aboard her included —
". . . Main sail Foresail two Catt Ropes main Sheet two running Tackles Main halliards a Piece of Spare Rope for
Sheats . . .".¹⁰

On the other hand the following taken from the Virginia Gazette, No. 119, for 3-10 March 1738, might well be
describing one of the many small single-masted vessels shown
in early American port scenes — "They went away in a
Shallop of about 19 Feet Keel, with a new Main Sail made
of the best Canvas, and her Fore Sail made of a Cloth a Size

thinner; her upper Works from the Bends are new; she is sheathed from the Bends to her Keel with Pine Plank; her upper Works paid with Turpentine; . . . Her Cabin not finished, but hath Windows; she has a new Deck laid upon old Beams; hath high Quarters, and a Counter, and built with a full Bow".

One hardly knows what to call the single-masted vessel shown in Figure 20. She appears on John Foster's 1677

Figure 20. Single-masted vessel. After Foster-Map of New England.

wood-cut map of New England and seems to have a boomless sprit mainsail and a triangular foresail.[11]

For an indeterminate period it is quite likely that size had a considerable influence on type terminology; the presence of a cuddy or a deck may also have been a factor. During the second half of the seventeenth century the smallest category was plain "boat," although the term was also used in a general way in referring to other craft. Boats seem to have been entirely open. As we have previously noted, the fishing shallops had cuddies to shelter their crews and were fitted with rooms. Sloops were the next step up the scale and, by the end of the century, usually decked in the north although local trade in the south favored open vessels. A definite size differential is borne out by Maryland records listing the shallops and sloops in use or under construction in 1697. Reports from eleven counties record the existence of 56 shallops and 70 sloops. Unfortunately, no dimensions are given and carrying capacities or burdens are listed for only 16 of the shallops and 32 of the sloops, but these can be considered as a fair sampling.[12]

All of the carrying capacities for the 16 shallops are given in hogsheads of tobacco. A hogshead in 1657 measured 43 inches in length and 26 inches in diameter over the head. In 1672 it was reckoned that an empty hogshead weighed 75 pounds and that one full of tobacco weighed 560 pounds. The smallest of the shallops could carry 10 hogsheads. Of the other 15 shallops two were rated at 30 hogsheads, one at 25, while the others ranged from 12 to 20.

As for the sloops, capacities for 24 of the 32 are given in hogsheads while tons burden are listed for the remainder. Two of the sloops, one from Talbot County and the other from Dorset County, are listed as carrying four hogsheads and for the latter, there is the note "under the deck." The four hogsheads for these two sloops may be in error as the smallest of the others was listed as "about 18 or 20 hogsheads;" the largest sloop could carry 70. Of the sloops rated by tons burden there were three of 45, four of 40, and one of 35 tons.

Including the Dorset County sloop only three of the 70 sloops are known to have been decked. It is unreasonable, however, to assume that all the others were open even though their use in the tobacco trade would make it likely. In the late seventeenth century open craft employed on inland waters of the English North American colonies were issued licenses by the local naval authorities. Decked vessels engaged in coastwise or overseas trading were issued a certificate of registry by the local authorities and the pertinent information on the certificate was forwarded to London to be incorporated in a master register of British vessels. As the tons burden of a vessel was a part of the information given on her certificate it is probable that the eight sloops for which a tonnage was given were substantial decked vessels.

In contrast with the number of sloops and shallops in Maryland, Governor Andros of Virginia reported in July 1697 only 15 sloops.[13] It is probable that there were many unreported small craft belonging to the various plantations.

The Massachusetts Archives contain extensive shipping records that are quite complete from 1697 to 1714 but which also include scattered information back to 1674.[14] These records consist of vessel registers, licenses to sail from Boston, fishing passports, permits to pass the Castle, and certificates issued in accordance with Rear-Admiral Byng's treaty with Algiers. Sloops — 560 named vessels — account for about 40% of the total of 1406 vessels listed. There are actually 965 entries for sloops but these include licenses to the same vessel for different voyages and many cases of re-registration because of change of owners.

On the other hand, in contrast to the Maryland records, there are but four shallops included in the total. *Joseph*, a round-sterned vessel of about 15 tons that had been captured from the French, was registered on 19 July 1704 and this is the only registration of a shallop. Licenses to sail from Boston were issued to three shallops between 17 December 1686 and 12 April 1689, the only period for which such information is available. In September 1687 *Ann* of Virginia, a 5-ton shallop with a crew of four sailed for Virginia, the 6-ton *Prudence* of Boston with three men cleared for Virbinia in October of the same year, and *James*, a 10-ton shallop owned in New York also with a crew of three, obtained a license to sail to New York in July 1688. An appraisement

of the latter turned up in the New York records for October
1688 — " . . . the hull with masts and standing rigging, main
yard and fore yard, anchor and cable £20, total £150."[15]
One open shallop was rebuilt in 1705 and converted to a decked sloop. This was *Flying Horse* which had a burden after
conversion of 20 tons, but there were also ordinary shallops
of the same size.

The above noted scarcity of shallops, however, is somewhat misleading. In the Chesapeake region shallops were employed largely for trading, hence required licenses and were
listed, while in New England this was not the case as shallops there were used primarily for fishing. How long the two-
masted square-rigged shallop continued in service in New
England waters is probably impossible to determine at this
late date — perhaps to the mid eighteenth century. There is
a definite record of two shallops so rigged in 1707. On 21
September of that year two shallops riding at anchor in
Winter Harbor, Maine, were attacked by about one hundred
and fifty Indians in fifty "canoos" who attempted to capture
them presumably for use in further depredations along the
coast and against the colonists' fishing fleets. The Indians
and their French backers were causing considerable trouble
along the New England coast during the latter part of the
seventeenth century and in the early years of the eighteenth.
The colonials, a total of eight men and one boy, consolidated
their forces in one shallop leaving the other temporarily to
the Indians who — " . . . no sooner had they taken possession
thereof, but they got their Mainsail atrip, before that our Men
could get theirs half mast high, and then put out their Oares,
which they joined with Paddles on each side; but having no
fargood, and their Boat a dull sailor, ours gained on them so
much, that they got twelve or thirteen Canoos ahead, with
Fishing-lines to tow them. But a breeze springing up, & the

Enemy making too near the Wind, (for want of a fargood) came to stays several times. . . ". The colonials apparently had the better shallop and a fargood, too, for they eventually were successful in their chase.[16]

The term *fargood* is the key to the fact that these two shallops were square-rigged, and this account is the earliest written use of the word yet found in the English language. In the basic rig of the Biscay shallop the presence or absence of a bowsprit determined whether the small foresail could be carried when the shallop was beating to windward as a bowsprit provided securing points for the tack and bowlines. The fargood was a spar that permitted the carrying of the foresail when beating without the need of a bowsprit. Defined

Figure 21. Fishing boat in 1727 showing 'fargood' on foresail.
After Morton Nance.

as a "spar bowline" the fargood was employed by Breton and
Cornish fishermen and it is shown in use on the foresail in
Figure 21. The derivation of fargood is unknown — in eastern Cornwall and in Devon it was *vargord* — but such a spar
was employed by the medieval Norse seamen who knew it
as the *beitiass* — the tacking boom.

Shallops, presumably square-rigged, were still employed for fishing in the 1720's. The Boston News-Letter for 9
July 1722 reported that two shallops and four schooners from
Marblehead were captured by pirates in the harbor of Port
Roseway, Nova Scotia. The entry for 10 July 1724 in the
journal of a voyage "In ye good Sloop *Sarah*" from the island
of Jersey to Cape Ann reads — " . . . at 4 this morning sound-
ed, found 65 fathom cors gray sand, got a cusk, saw two
shallops & one Skooner of Marblehead, and they told us that
Cape Sable Bore of them N.N.W. about 15 Leagues".[17]
While in earlier days there are references to Salem shallops
fishing off the coast of Maine (Mohegan was a popular base
of operations), the locations for these later shallops indicate a
somewhat more substantial vessel. Figure 22 is adapted

Figure 22. Shallop, 1725. After Burgis.

from the William Burgis view of Boston that was published in 1725 by William Price; it undoubtedly represents one of the square-rigged shallops.

Regarding the Massachusetts sloops, in keeping with the general tradition that most early small craft were basically double-enders as such a form was easier to build, we find that the earliest sloops listed in the previously mentioned records had round sterns. The oldest is the 15-ton *Rose* of Boston which was built in Salem in 1674; presumably she was decked. The oldest open round-sterned sloop is the 15-ton *Speedwell* of Lynn built at that port in 1677. The decked round-sterned sloop *Flying Horse* of Boston has already been mentioned as having been rebuilt from an open shallop. Omitting this vessel and round-sterned sloops captured from the French, there is a total of 14 round-sterned sloops, half of which were built prior to 1688; the last of such sloops in these records was constructed at Plymouth in 1712.

A total of 23 open square-sterned sloops were registered, eight of which were built before 1700. These were not all small craft as one might think. The smallest is the 12-ton *Industry* of Boston, built there in 1685, while the largest are two 36-ton sloops — *Mary* of Hartford, built in Hingham in 1702, and *Endeavour* of Boston, built in Scituate in 1703. The last of the open square-sterned sloops in the existing registration list is *Blossom* of Boston, a 30-ton vessel built in Marshfield in 1713. Considering that in 1687 a 4-ton sloop was trading between Boston and the Carolinas and 6-tonners sailed to Bermuda and the Leeward Islands, we can only guess as to the employment of these large open sloops in New England. These are references to cargoes of hay and wood carried in open boats — stone is another possibility. The Boston News-Letter for 5 March 1704/5 advertised for sale a fishing sloop that could — " . . . carry six Cord of Wood without taking down her rooms".

At the other end of the scale are the 80-ton sloops, *St. Antony*, a square-sterned vessel of Boston that was issued an Algiers certificate in 1711, and *Amiable* of London that had been captured from the French in 1696. Next in size are one 75-ton sloop, two 70-tonners, and a number at 60 tons. The great majority, however, are in the 20- to 40-ton range. Details of large sloops before 1700 are scarce but the contract for a sloop built in Portsmouth, New Hampshire, in 1694 provides a few.[18] She measured 41 feet on the keel and 16 feet 9 inches in breadth. The contract specified that in reckoning her tonnage half of the breadth would represent the depth and the divisor should be 95 — the tonnage works out to be slightly over 60. Her actual depth in hold was 7 feet 6 inches. She had a two-foot rise aft from the main deck to the quarter deck and a one-foot rise forward. Her bulwarks amidships were 30 inches deep and were cut for four gun ports on each side. She was to have been constructed—" . . . of good sound seasoned white oake timber and plank except where Pine may be more convenient . . .". No details of her rig are given.

Some details of the rig of the 28-ton sloop *Supply* can be gleaned from an inventory dated 15 March 1691 made after completion of her first voyage. She had a keel length of 34 feet, a breadth inside her planking of 12 feet 6 inches, and a hold depth of 6 feet. Her listed spars are the mast, boom, square sail yard, bowsprit, and flying jib boom. For sails she had a mainsail, foresail, jib, flying jib, and spritsail. By way of auxiliary power she had two oars "nigh 30 feet long".[19]

Considering the configuration of what is presently accepted as a sloop rig, there are some unusual points about these details. The spritsail, assuming it to be a square sail under the bowsprit, is uncommon. There is scattered Dutch and English pictorial evidence for such a sail on single-masted fore-and-aft rigged vessels but North American examples have not yet been found. From the normal point of view there are three omissions — a spritsail yard, an upper spar (gaff) to support the fore-and-aft mainsail, and a square sail. Fortrey wrote in 1675 that smack sails were "boomed or spritted" aloft, i.e. they had what today is called a long gaff with no spar at the bottom, hence "boom" in the inventory might mean a long gaff. There are examples in the Burgis view of Boston of the boomless gaff sail and the fore-and-aft spritsail which cannot completely be ruled out in this case; the mainsail in the inventory might be the square course.

✿✿✿✿✿✿✿✿✿✿✿✿✿✿✿✿✿✿✿✿✿✿✿✿✿✿✿✿✿✿✿✿

CHAPTER V

Two - Mast Boats

BUT WHAT of the two-masted fore-and-aft rigged Dutch sloops and jaghts? There are so many two-masted fore-and-aft rigged craft without headsails shown in early eighteenth-century views and maps of North American seaports that we can be sure these basic types did not cease to exist when the English took over the North American colonies of the Netherlands, only to be re-invented at a later time. After the term sloop became common as the designation of single-masted fore-and-aft rigged vessels of a variety of sizes, there was apparently no word in the English language suitable for the two-masters. Ashley noted that in North America, even after the supposed invention of the schooner at Gloucester in 1713, the term sloop was generally applied for some time to all vessels rigged with gaff sails. He also stated that until about 1750 the English called a small open schooner a shallop and a large decked one a sloop.¹

Blanckley's definition of a sloop has been quoted but his sketch from which Figure 23 was taken shows a square-sterned vessel with but one mast carrying a boomed mainsail supported by a relatively short gaff, a foresail, and a jib. His

Figure 23. British sloop. After Blanckley.

shallop of the early eighteenth century was — " . . . a small
light Vessell with only a small Main & Fore Mast & Lugsails
to hall up & let down on occasion . . . "; she is shown in Figure
24. These lugsails, however, bear little resemblance to the
presently accepted shapes of such sails and would be called
today boomless sails with long gaffs. Obviously such a definition could not have been applied in New England as the
fishing shallops there had the two-masted square rig with a
single, deep, narrow, square sail on each mast. The only
term left for the two-masted fore-and-afters was just "boat"
with sometimes a place name as a descriptive adjective, a

Figure 24. British shallop. After Blanckley.

practice which became more prevalent in later days. And in New England, at least, small two-masted fishing craft remained just boats until the last days of the commercial use of sail.

One of the earliest of such "boats" in colonial records was that known as the Bermudas boat, which had two loose-footed boomless triangular sails laced to well-raked masts. Perhaps the earliest representation of such a boat was published in 1671, Figure 25. [2] By well established tradition it had a Dutch origin as the governor of Bermuda in 1620 — ". . . imployed a Dutch carpenter of the former Dutch wrack to build Boates".[3] The high stern of the Dutch sloop of 1629, Figure 16, is absent but the other features are there.[4] It is, of course, impossible from the sketch of the Bermuda boat to determine whether she had a square or a sharp stern.

By 1689 the Bermudas boat was employed for fishing in Boston waters and was then half decked. [5] Fortrey in his

Figure 25. Bermudas boat, 1671. After Morris.

discussion of various types of sails in 1675 commented adversely on the loose-footed "Bermoodes saile," noting that in running before the wind it could not extend beyond the boat's side and that it was not convenient, "yare" is his actual word, for tacking as the sheet had to be shifted from side to side each time the boat came about. In his opinion the boomed short-gaff sail was to be preferred over the spritsail of the hoy, the long-gaff smack sail, and the "Bermoodes saile".[6]

The two-masted Bermuda rig if not the hull, by whatever name it may have borne later, had a long life. Examples may be found in the 1717 Burgis view of New York, a map of New York of about 1730, various representations of Philadelphia around the middle of the eighteenth century, a shipyard scene in Maryland of about 1760, a view of Boston in 1773, and a waterfront scene of Duxbury, Massachusetts, of about 1800. There are also representations of the rig carried by open boats in Dutch and English views of the late eighteenth century. Considering the tradition of a Dutch background for the loose-footed triangular sail, it is a strange quirk of fate that it should have picked up the Bermuda name.

A boat stolen in Rhode Island in 1795 probably had this two-masted Bermuda rig as she had the provisions for the shifting of sheets to which Fortrey objected. An advertisement that appeared in *The Newport Mercury* for 2 June 1795 read in part — "STOLEN from the Subscriber on Saturday Night, May 9th, a double-bottom CEDAR BOAT, 19 Feet Keel, Green Bottom, black Wale, and white Hanks, Name on Her Stern, *Republican* — very long headed Nails for Clinches thro' her Waist; Bullet Headed Nails in her Stern; an Iron Clamp with a Brass Sheave at her Stern [Stem?] for heaving up her anchor; at her foremast Head, a blue Vane; she had two Staples in each Quarter for shifting her Sheets; her starboard Stern Sheet new, not painted; she has a small Scuttle for a Pump besides, and for bailing abaft; some new Patches in her Bulk Head, not painted; a Cable of about 30 fathoms; an Anchor, with Iron Stock about 40 lb. her Blocks all bushed with Iron Pins; her Sails Russia Duck; she had five square Pieces of Pig Iron, 450 Weight, and Stones for Ballast; and a joint Cover over her Ballast, not painted, with a Lock to it; Cod Lines, Hooks, and Leads, and a Compass on board, with many other Things not mentioned ....".[7] This is a very complete description of a square-sterned, clinker-built, partly-decked, two-masted fishing boat.

We have seen that by the early part of the eighteenth century the New England fishing shallops had become substantial vessels suitable for the offshore fisheries. Such craft as the Bermudas boat along with open sloops had replaced the shallops for inshore work. A hint of this change is found in a petition in 1694 to the General Court of Massachusetts by some of the inhabitants of Marblehead — " . . . Praying that they may be eased of the duty of Tunage for their Fishing Shallops and that they may onely be considered and taken in as other ratable Estate". In the record of the vote by the House of Representatives approving the petition the words "Fishing Shallops" were carefully crossed out and replaced by "open Boats".[9]

Many of these open boats had exactly the two-masted rig of the Dutch *speeljaght* — two masts with the main raking more than the fore, the fore mast being the shorter, and two short-gaff sails. Both of these were loosefooted but the main was fitted with a boom. Figure 26, a good example of such craft, is taken from "A North East View of the Great Town of Boston" attributed to Willam Burgis in 1723. Her rigging would have been the simplest possible — no shrouds, no stays, a single halyard for each sail, double sheets for the foresail, and a single sheet for the main.

A very similar little boat, open except for a cuddy forward, was described in the *Virginia Gazette* for 28 September 1739—"On Friday Night, the 21st of this Instant September, one James Hobbs, a Ship-Carpenter, stole a Boat from Newport-Nuse, on James River, belonging to the Subscriber, and went away with her; and neither Man nor Boat is yet heard of by him. The Boat is about 15 Feet Keel, has two Masts, is paid inside and out with Pitch, has a large Grapling, with one Flook bent almost to the other; a Washboard fix'd on each Side with small Timbers upon an old Gunhill, an Iron Horse for the Mainsheet to traverse upon, with a staple at each end . . . ". This little boat would not have been more than 20 feet in length over-all.

Figure 26. Two-mast boat, 1723. After Burgis.

Such craft were widely known as "two-mast boats".
Like the shallops, which had developed from open boats to
boats with cuddies and finally to offshore vessels, the two-
mast boat went through a similar evolution with the passing
of time. Many retained the old sharp stern as it was not only
easier and cheaper to build but it was considered more sea-

worthy than the square stern. The square stern, which had become common on ships' boats by the late seventeenth century, gave more deck space aft in the same over-all length or conversely allowed a shorter length for equal deck space. In 1733 there was announced for sale in Boston — " . . . a Large Two mast Boat, well fitted and deck'd, with two Suits of Sails, a good Road and Anchor, with an Iron Hearth".[9] An advertisement in 1757 offered — " . . Two Pinck-Stern'd two Mast Boats — one ditto square-sterned, with Masts, Rigging and Sails . . . all lying in the Town-Dock above the Bridge. One other Pinck-stern'd two mast Boat, with rigging and sails, lying at Mr. Thomas Bentley's, Boat-builder, at the North End".[10] For all practical purposes such boats were the then up-dated and current versions of the old shallop carrying fore-and-aft instead of square rigs. It seems unusual that although William Burgis showed a two-mast boat under sail in his little-known 1723 "North East View . . . . of Boston" and another under oars in his 1729 view of Castle William in Boston Harbor, no such craft is shown in either his 1717 view of New York or his well-known 1725 view of Boston where we would expect to find examples of the type.

Along with the growth in size of the two-mast boat there were the inevitable changes in rig. The very short gaffs of the Dutch sails — still in evidence in the 1723 Burgis view of Boston mentioned above — were replaced by longer and longer gaffs, the foremast approached the main in height, and the foresail became larger but it remained boomless in most localities until well after the Revolution. The change to the longer gaffs may have occurred earlier in the southern colonies than in the northern ones. An idealized picture of the waterfront of Philadelphia, painted about 1720 by Peter Cooper of whom practically nothing is known, shows two two-masted fore-and-aft rigged craft without headsails; both have longer gaffs in proportion to the feet of the sails than do the various single-masted vessels in the picture.[11]

Even about 50 years later Boston boats still seem to have relatively short gaffs. A painting by Christian Remick of the landing of two British regiments at Boston on 1 October 1768 shows the originals of the sketches in Figure 27. An item in

Figure 27. Two-mast boats, 1768. After Remick.

the *Boston Gazette* for 21 January 1782 gives a good description of just such a boat — "Stolen and carried off last Wednesday night, from Rainsford Island by a number of British prisoners, the State Hospital Two Mast Boat. She is 23 feet keel, a long cuddy with a fireplace and cabins in it, one anchor and cable, a new foresail, her mainsail old, a new boom not tarred and her sides painted yellow". The cuddies are quite prominent on the boats in the Remick painting; the term "cabin" in those days meant what today we would call a bunk.

The Remick boats have brown hulls — probably intended to represent oiled wood — while the cuddies forward and the gunwales are red. Colors of another two-mast boat are given in the *Boston Gazette* for 8 September 1777—"Taken away from the End of Tilestone's Wharf, on Wednesday

Night last, a lap Streak Two Mast Boat, painted Black and Yellow, a lower streak Chocolate Color, the Masts painted Yellow, the top of the Fore-Mast Black, the top of the Main-Mast not black, a Graplin on board instead of an Anchor".

In view of the small sizes of some of the eighteenth-century schooners — a vessel of ten tons in one case and "something under 20 Feet Keel" in another as examples — the continued existence of these relatively large gaff-rigged two-mast boats without headsails seems surprising today. We are liable to assume that the natural thing would be to add a bowsprit and set a staysail forward. The fact is, however, that the two-mast boats were quite satisfactory for the services in which they were employed. Today when a sailor's choice of boat is influenced by arbitrary rating rules rather than the fact that he must earn his living with it, few know how these old types could perform. Some proof of their qualities has been gained from a reconstruction of a two-mast boat that has been sailing and sailing well in Chesapeake waters since July 1960.[12]

With an overall length of 28 feet 10 inches and a maximum breadth to the outside of the normal planking of 7 feet 11¼ inches, this boat is intended to represent a plantation boat of about 1725. Modern cruising comforts are provided by a removable house which shelters four berths, a head and a stove platform; a reproduction of an old sea chest in her ample cockpit hides a gasoline engine. Her two loose-footed sails are of the short gaff "shoulder-of-mutton" type with the main only having a boom. As her load draft in cruising condition is only about 30 inches she carries leeboards to improve her sailing ability to windward. Figure 28 is a sketch of her under sail.

The lines of a similar but slightly smaller boat are shown in Figure 29. Except for the arrangement of the deadwood

Figure 28. The *Aviza* Shallop, 1960.

aft to accommodate a propeller, these lines are typical of early eighteenth-century boats as shown by examples in the files of England's National Maritime Museum and other similar sources. Of the traditional cod's head and mackerel's tail form, they were developed by the procedure known as "whole-molding" in which only two molds are employed to shape the sections.[13]

The final developments during the nineteenth century of the small craft which were in use until the internal combustion engine replaced sail in the commercial inshore fisheries are fully covered in H. I. Chappell's *American Small Sailing Craft*. But we must follow our two-mast boat into the vessel category although it was still called only a boat.

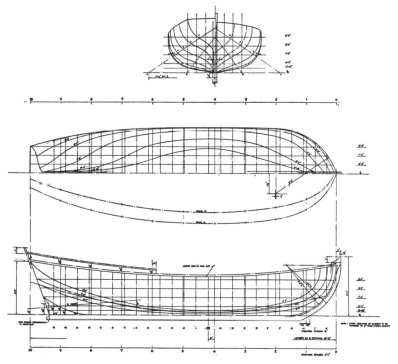

Figure 29. Lines for reproduction of an early 18th century boat.

CHAPTER VI

Chebacco Boats

I T COMMONLY has been assumed by those not closely associated with marine activities that vessels for a given service have been improved gradually through the years in size, speed and all desirable qualities. The records, however, show that the size and qualities of vessels have varied considerably depending upon the international and local conditions that affected their employment.

On 13 May 1799 the Reverend Mr. William Bentley, pastor of the East Church in Salem, Massachusetts, wrote in his diary concerning a boat trip around Cape Ann— "As we opened the coves we had an opportunity of seeing the fashion of mooring Boats commonly called Jebacco boats because built first in that part of Ipswich. They perforate a large stone & raise a tree with its roots & stripped of its branches, & then slide the stone over the stock of the tree upon the root. The root prevents the stone from a seperation & this is carried & sunk in a convenient place the top remaining like a post above water." He noted that there were at that time about 300 "Jebacco" boats employed in the fisheries out of Cape Ann's coves and harbors; about half of them sailed from Sandy Bay, the present Rockport.[1] Eighteen years later on a visit to what is now the town of Essex he wrote — " . . . the sight of Jebacco boats building for the bay fishery not only at every landing place but in the yards of the farmers some distances from the shores, as a novelty was very impressive".[2]

This popularity of the Jebacco or Chebacco boat, to use the customary spelling, was one of the results of the American Revolution; later the War of 1812 had a similar effect. To aid the New England and mainly the Massachusetts fishermen who had become impoverished by the war, the Congress granted on 4 July 1789 a bounty of five cents per quintal of dried fish or barrel of pickled fish exported.[3] In 1791 the Massachusetts General Court petitioned for more support from the federal government and on 9 February 1792 a payment varying from one to two and a half dollars per ton depending on size was granted to vessels that were engaged in the cod fisheries for a period of at least four months per year. Three-eighths of this grant went to the owner of a vessel while the remainder was divided among her crew.[4] Under these bounties fishing was resumed on the Grand Banks of Newfoundland with such old schooners as had survived the war, but in general the fishermen could not afford to build new vessels of the size necessary for the Banks fisheries. They turned to the inshore fisheries which could be pursued with smaller vessels — the local ledges, the coast of Maine, and even to the Bay of Chaleur and the Labrador coast where fishing rights had been obtained by the peace treaty. By 1808 about three-quarters of the dried fish exported from Massachusetts came from the Bay and Labrador fisheries — less than one-quarter were taken from the Grand Banks which required larger vessels and more expensive gear.[5]

About five miles up a narrow, winding, tidal stream from Ipswich Bay is a boat yard in which there stands a metal sign bearing the following:

SHIPYARD OF 1668
IN 1668 THE TOWN GRANTED
THE ADJACENT ACRE OF LAND "TO
THE INHABITANTS OF IPSWICH FOR
A YARD TO BUILD VESSELS AND TO
EMPLOY WORKMEN FOR THAT END".
THE SHIPBUILDING INDUSTRY HAS
CONTINUED UNINTERRUPTEDLY IN
ESSEX SINCE THAT DATE.

In 1668 this acre of land was part of the Chebacco parish
of the town of Ipswich. First settled in 1634 this parish was
legally established in 1819 as the Town of Essex, now famous as the birthplace of hundreds of schooners for Gloucester
and other fishing ports.[6] The land of the parish was not particularly suitable for agriculture and its inhabitants turned
to the sea and fishing for their livelihood. Excellent stands
of virgin timber provided the materials from which they built
their own boats, which were restricted in size by economic
considerations and the limitations of the river. The later large
schooners built in yards along the river were towed out in
light condition and rigged elsewhere. The first sawmill was
erected on the river in 1656 and by 1667 three were in opera-
tion.[7]

According to tradition a Burnham built the first boat
in the parish in 1659 or 1660;[8] Burnham later became the
most common name in Essex. The following summer a man
and a boy, also Burnhams, sailed her to Damariscove Island
in Maine for a fare of fish.[9] It became the common practice
after a summer of fishing to sell a boat in the fall and to build
another during the winter. This first boat was constructed,
also according to tradition, not in a yard on the river's bank,
but in the garret of a house one end of which had to be cut
away to get her out.[10] As the Reverend Mr. Bentley noted,

this practice of building away from the river continued in later times. In the year 1838 one of the last and perhaps the largest of the Chebacco boats so built was constructed in the back yard of the home of her builder in South Essex: *Columbia*, which was about 60 feet long and measured over 65 tons.[11] The distance to the water in some cases was more than a mile; for the journey a boat was loaded on two sets of wheels and drawn by ten or twelve yoke of oxen. The wheels were run into the river at low tide and the boat floated off as the water rose.[12]

The previously mentioned Massachusetts Archives list only 14 vessels as having been built in the town of Ipswich during the period they cover and only three, all sloops, were specifically noted as having been built in the Chebacco parish. These were the 18-ton square-sterned *Mayflower* of Salem built in 1698, the 12-ton round-sterned *Industry* of Boston constructed in the following year, and *Beginning* of Boston, a 30-ton square-sterned vessel built in 1708. Details of a very few others may be found in court records. This activity or rather the lack of it emphasizes the fact that Chebacco-built craft were in the main just fishing vessels for which there are no records.

In all probability the early boats, such as that built and sailed by the Burnhams to Damariscove, were the typical shallops of their day. By the time reasonably reliable information becomes available over a century later, the basic Chebacco boat was a sharp-sterned vessel carrying a two-masted fore-and-aft rig without headsails. A peculiar feature was that her low bulwarks or rails were carried aft to meet behind the head of the rudder — a pink. No one can tell at what stage in history these bulwarks were given the sharp kickup at their junction which made them serviceable as a support for the main boom as well as a seat-of-ease for the crew. Forward the stem was quite prominent and the bulwarks often were not attached to it — it served as a bitt over which the eye of a line from the previously described mooring was dropped. Because of this feature these craft were often called "Ram's-head boats".

Also locally known as "pinkeys," or "pinkies" to use the modern spelling, because of the construction of their sterns, the Chebacco boats of around 1800 ranged in size from 12 to 25 tons burthen and carried crews of three. Their characteristics were the same as those of a larger vessel of some 20 to 30 years later as recalled by an old seaman — "At one time he used to go coasting in what would now [1882] be thought a small craft, but what they considered a monster, an old-fashioned standing-room pinkey of forty-two tons, with timber heads coming up along her sides six or eight inches, around which a plank was bent to serve as bulwarks — then called a waist. She had fore-and-aft standing rooms, a fore-cuddy with a brick chimney and fireplace, carried fore-and-aft sails, and was without shrouds or bowsprit. She had hemp, or what was then called Raven's duck sails — cotton duck was then unknown — and carried a scout horn to wet them down when the wind was moderate. They used to coast along shore, carrying corn and lumber, and once went as far south as Charleston."[13] Lest this last seem to indicate limited capabilities let it be noted that Chebacco boats also voyaged to the West Indies and regularly fished in the Gulf of St. Lawrence. They had a good reputation for seaworthiness and fast sailing.[14]

One of the earliest indications of the form of a Chebacco boat is the model in the Smithsonian Institution upon which Figure 30 is based. It is considered to be an old fisherman-built model representing a boat of the late 1790's about 38 feet long on deck with a breadth of 11 feet 4 inches and a

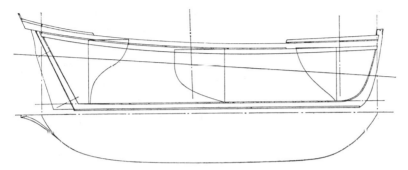

Figure 30. Chebacco boat, ca. 1790. After Chapelle.

depth of 5 feet 6 inches; she would have measured about 21 tons. Using this model as a guide and employing actual Custom House dimensions, H. I. Chapelle has reconstructed the lines of a typical small Chebacco boat which were published in the United States National Museum Bulletin 219 — *The National Watercraft Collection*. These lines show a long straight keel having considerable drag, a slightly curved and raked stem, and a sharply raked straight sternpost. The midsection has a straight rising floor, a high and hard bilge, and practically straight topsides. The entrance is short but relatively sharp and the extreme forward sections are V-shaped. The run is long and well formed. Other sources indicated that in many cases the stem had more curvature than on this model.

The model's arrangement corroborates the old seaman's description of the larger coasting Chebacco "pinkey". The length of the cuddy forward is about one-quarter of the overall length and its deck is level with the top of the bulwarks or rails which run aft and meet behind the rudder head. The companion hatch is on the centerline, the chimney for the fireplace is to starboard, and there is a water barrel to port. There are two standing rooms for fishing with a fish hatch immediately abaft each; a third standing room is provided aft for the helmsman. The mainmast is stepped slightly abaft the midlength on deck while the foremast is in the eyes of the model, leaving barely enough room for a small windlass between it and the head of the stem. On some boats the windlass was just abaft the foremast. A single log pump is located between the after fish hatch and the helmsman's standing room.[15]

The cuddy of such a boat, depending upon its size, would have been crowded with three or four berths and a brick fireplace. The chimney to the deck might also have been of brick or perhaps of wood well plastered on the inside. Above deck there was a small portable section of wood that usually was of little use in carrying off smoke. It has been said that fishermen in the smoky cuddies of Chebacco boats first found that wood smoke improved the flavor of the halibut hung there to dry.[16]

Just how an earlier Chebacco boat may have looked is anyone's guess and Figure 31 is mine. The curved stem, absent in Figure 30, is a typical seventeenth and eighteenth century shape — it appears on the Smithsonian model of a square-sterned Chebacco boat to be discussed in the following paragraph. Representing one of the smaller boats of about 11 tons burden, her lines were developed by the whole-molded process which was still the standard method for designing small craft in the eighteenth century, although the system had been much modified for large vessels. Her form is essentially that of an enlarged ship's boat of the mid-eighteenth century but with a little more deadrise which may not be justified. Living conditions aboard such a boat would have been cramped indeed and her use would have been limited to short voyages out of Cape Ann's coves and harbors. Being a small boat she has no bulwarks and her cuddy ap-

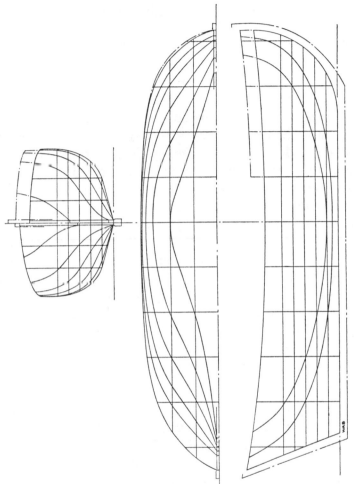

Figure 31. Possible form of an early Chebacco boat.

pears as a raised forecastle as on Christian Remick's boats, Figure 27.

Although the sharp or pink-sterned Chebacco boat was the favored model at the time of the Reverend Mr. Bentley's visit, there was also a square-sterned Chebacco boat that was commonly known as a "dogbody". The origin of this designation is lost in time. Generally speaking, dogbodies were a little smaller than the pink-sterned boats as the square stern gave the same amount of deck room on a shorter length. Again probably the earliest evidence is a Smithsonian model which, if taken at a scale of ½ inch to the foot, represents a vessel having a length overall of about 36 feet and a breadth of 11 feet 6 inches. She would have measured about 20 tons. While the lines of this model have not been published, its appearance indicates that, although deeper, the form is very similar to the boat shown in Figure 29. The stern, however, departs from the simple transom of a small boat and there is an overhanging middle transom with a raking flat upper transom abaft the rudder. Her fittings are essentially the same as those of the pink-sterned model, but her windlass is located abaft her foremast.[17]

A shorter description might be that the Chebacco boat, in both the pink-sterned and dogbody versions, was simply the then current and favored version of the two-mast boat. The smaller sizes often had no bulwarks, only low rails, while the larger craft were usually fully decked with no standing rooms. Schoolboy sketches indicate that the bulwarks of Chebacco boats were usually painted black with one or more white stripes. Black, green, and even red were used for the topsides; the upper part of the stem that formed the mooring bitt was commonly red. According to the same sketches, both the fore and main sails were fitted with booms but were loose footed at least until the mid 1830's. The gaffs of both sails were long with separate peak and throat halliards.

Being but developments of the earlier two-mast boats, which in turn were the descendants of the colonial shallops, construction of the two Chebacco types was not limited to the Chebacco parish or the neighboring Cape Ann from which so many sailed. Similar boats were built to the southward, particularly in the Massachusetts towns between Boston and Cape Cod, and to the eastward in Maine and Canada's Maritime Provinces. As both the pink-sterned and dogbody Chebaccos were built in increasingly larger sizes with the passing of time, their once easily handled rig became heavier and harder to work. They were eventually supplanted in the larger sizes by the schooner-rigged vessels of the same basic forms that had existed all during their development. There is evidence that the pink-sterned Chebacco boat lasted longer in Massachusetts waters than the dogbody but that the later was employed on the Hudson River and on rivers in Maine well into the second half of the nineteenth century. Developments of both versions lasted even longer in Canada.

❀❀❀❀❀❀❀❀❀❀❀❀❀❀❀❀❀❀❀❀❀❀❀❀❀❀❀

Chapter VII

Chebacco Boat Descendants

URING the nineteenth century the communities of
Camden, Rockport, Rockland, and Thomaston in the
State of Maine were widely known for the production of lime.
The limestone from hundreds of quarries was hauled to the
shore-line where it was burned into lime in wood-burning
kilns which at one time numbered well over a hundred in
Rockland alone. Although wood-burned lime was considered
the best, coal and oil eventually supplanted wood as fuel, but
during the heyday of these operations about thirty cords of
wood were required for one burning in each kiln.[1]

The transportation of cordwood for the kilns employed
more vessels than the shipping of the finished product to
market. All sorts of craft loaded wood at about every possible landing place along the coast of Maine from early spring
until ice closed the harbors. Many old coasters, no longer
suitable for voyages to Atlantic coast ports or the West Indies — "Often in charge of sick or superannuated captains,
with mere boys or half-wits for crew . . . ended their days
as kiln-wooders from nearby points".[2] In recent years similar
craft carried pulp wood from the islands to paper mills on
the mainland.

92

Most of the vessels employed in this wood trade hailed
from ports in Maine but a fair proportion of the fuel came
from New Brunswick in the Saint John woodboats, more
popularly known as the "Johnny woodboats" or just "Jakes".
A sketch of one under sail is shown in Figure 32. The name

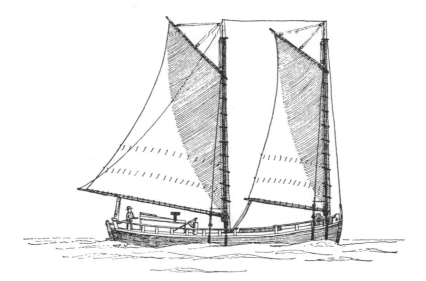

Figure 32. Saint John wood boat under sail.

derived from the fact that this unique type of vessel was built
almost exclusively on the lower Saint John River and its tributaries. The basic "Johnny woodboat" had a two-masted
fore-and-aft rig without bowsprit or headsail. One explanation given for the use of this rig was that— " . . . they often
loaded wood in such remote sylvan spots that bowsprits were
too likely to get mixed up with trees on the steep banks".[3]
A more logical explanation was that with the huge deck loads
usually carried a staysail would have been difficult to work.[4]
An even more telling reason may be that the ancestor of the

type was so rigged and as the rig proved satisfactory in service there was no need to change — the "Johnny woodboat"
in form and rig was a direct development of the dogbody
Chebacco boat. Some of the late nineteenth-century woodboats, however, were fitted with a bowsprit and a single
headsail; sailmaker's sketches show that a few were altered
from the orginal rig.

Many Loyalists migrated from the New England and
other colonies to Canada's Maritime Provinces at the time
of the American Revolution and either took with them or built
after settling down the types of small craft familiar to them.
As early as 1764, however, the trading company of Simonds,
Hazen, and White was established at the mouth of New
Brunswick's Saint John River to carry on trade with New
England. In November 1783 this company decided to build
two boats to bring wood to market — "Each boat was to be
undecked, carry a crew of two, and have a capacity of about
eight cords". While we can only surmise that these were dogbodies it is a fact that — "the sailboats which brought wood
and country produce to Saint John during the early nineteenth century were known as Chebacco boats" and the fact
that the woodboats had square sterns points to the dogbody
origin.[5]

Of course, not all the woodboats were engaged in carrying cordwood to the Maine lime-kilns. Other employment included the transportation of cut lumber from the
sawmills on the river down to ships in the harbor of Saint
John for shipment overseas. Some of the better boats carried such cargoes directly to the many New England ports;
occasionally they ventured as far south as Philadelphia. Still
other cargoes were timber and knees for the Saint John shipyards, cordwood to heat the homes of Saint John's residents,
hay, and even coal from the fields far up the river. A few

well equipped boats operated for years, even after the advent
of the steamboats, carrying passengers and general freight
on the river.[6]

The wood carrying trade required nothing fancy and
the average "Johnny woodboat" was considered the least expensive craft of its size ever constructed on the western shores
of the Atlantic.[7] Carvel planking was the rule and the poorer
boats were constructed almost entirely of spruce. Because of
the rough handling they received, ten years was considered
a long life. The better boats had birch or some other hard-
wood for planking below the water-line, while the topsides
and deck were planked with spruce. The keel, keelson, stem,
stern, knees, and stanchions were of hackmatack, the masts
were of white pine, and spruce served for the other members.[8]
Such boats had a longer life, the record being at least 46
years — *Emperor* of 31 tons, built in Kingston, New Brunswick, in 1843, was still registered in 1889. The last of the
"Johnny woodboats", *Maggie-Alice*, was broken up in 1930
after a career of 33 years.[9]

A woodboat usually carried a large deck load and her
sails had to be reefed so as to swing above the cargo; when
loaded, the deck amidships was often under water. Leaks
really did not matter as the cargo in the hold would keep
the boat afloat and it was said that occasionally a woodboat
sailed into port with the helmsman standing knee deep in
water. The deck loads of cordwood or cut lumber were often
so high the helmsman had to be directed by a crew member
stationed on top of the load forward.[10]

For years the hulls received no more protection than
a coating of tar or pitch — paint was considered a needless
luxury. When paint was finally employed on the later boats,
black was the predominant color with rails and bulwarks of
another or combination of colors. Some, however, had dark

green topsides while a very few were painted white. In the early days the sails were treated with red ocher, but as there was no proof that this really preserved the sails, the practice did not last.[11]

While the Saint John woodboat was a development of the dogbody Chebacco boat, there were, of course, as with the latter, no standard sizes or proportions. Some representative dimensions and proportions of each type are given in the following table:

DOGBODY CHEBACCO BOATS

	Length	Breadth	Depth	Tonnage	L/B	D/B
Raven						
1795	35.75 ft.	11.75 ft.	5.67 ft.	$20\frac{11}{95}$	3.04	0.483
Patriot						
1795	40.00	12.50	5.42	$22\frac{15}{95}$	3.20	0.434
Alert						
1804	38.25	11.00	5.92	$21\frac{66}{95}$	3.48	0.538
Talent						
1834	40.50	11.92	5.75	$24\frac{5}{95}$	3.40	0.482

SAINT JOHN WOODBOATS

	Length	Breadth	Depth	Tonnage	L/B	D/B
Emperor						
1843	55.9	15.4	5.6	$42\frac{34}{95}$ (31)	3.63	0.364
Bride						
1854	68.5	19.9	6.1	$72\frac{26}{95}$ (64)	3.44	0.307
Comrade						
1868	76.7	26.5	7.0	$118\frac{68}{95}$ (77)	2.89	0.264
Nina						
1879	36.0	13.8	4.0	$16\frac{10}{95}$ (11)	2.61	0.290
Josie F.						
1884	78.8	27.6	7.2	$130\frac{18}{95}$ (99)	2.86	0.261

The dimensions in the table are taken from official records. To permit comparison, tonnages have been calculated for the woodboats by the formula used for the tonnages of the dogbodies — their official Canadian tonnages in 1889 are given in parentheses. An examination of the length/breadth and depth/breadth ratios shows that the woodboats became relatively beamier and shallower as the nineteenth century progressed. Perhaps this is an indication of an increasing size of deck loads. As might be expected the smallest woodboat, *Nina*, is the beamiest of all in relation to her length.

From the original dogbody Chebacco boat, the woodboat grew rapidly in size, the tonnage of the average boat in 1815 being about twice that of the 1783 boat. From 1815 to 1825 there was another size increase and by 1830 the general features of the Saint John woodboat had become established.[12] The decade of the 1830's holds the record for the greatest number launched — 82 boats — after which the numbers slowly fell; only six were built between 1900 and 1917.[13] In 1889 there were 82 woodboats in commission and the most popular size was in the 60- to 70-ton range measured according to the Canadian rules. The following is the distribution of sizes:

Tonnage	10-20	20-30	30-40	40-50	50-60	60-70	70-80	80-90	90-100
No. of boats	3	3	9	5	9	22	17	11	3

The lines of a typical Saint John woodboat are given in Figure 33; they were taken from an old half model that served for the building of nine boats. Generally speaking, the woodboat was a shallow-draft keel vessel having little deadrise, a very full bow, and a long fine run, features which are well shown in these lines. The maximum section was located well forward of the half length. In spite of the shallow draft, there is no record that centerboards were ever fitted, but the boats were given deep outside keels. The curved stem with tumble-home and the outboard rudder with an outside sternpost were typical features. Many woodboats were fitted with bilge keels so as to keep them upright when they

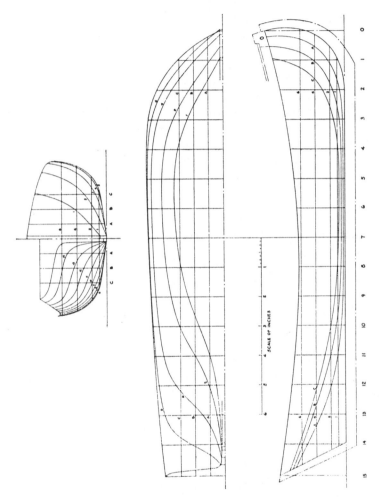

Figure 33. Lines of Saint John wood boat.

grounded out between Saint John's 30-foot tides. The shallow depth of the average hulls made them easy to load and unload over the side — carts could be driven alongside when they were grounded.

The seemingly clumsy form of the typical woodboat led to a fair amount of ridicule. Some Maine coast Yankees claimed that — ". . . the woodboats were built on the ice and in the spring were simply sawed off at the desired length".[14] There is also the oft-quoted dialogue between two skippers: "Where's the other one?" "What other one?" "Why, the one they turned to and sawed that one off'n!"[15] In spite of its strange appearance to modern eyes accustomed to the long slim forms of present day yachts, the only sail-propelled craft with which most sailors have had experience, the woodboat's form, essentially that of a seventeenth-century boat, was quite satisfactory in smooth waters and even moderate seas. The woodboats commonly reached speeds of nine or ten knots on the river and gave even better performance out in the Bay of Fundy. All along the New England coast the "Johnny woodboats" were generally known as better than average sailers. One boat, *Comrade*, whose particulars are given above, reputedly beat a Boston pilot boat in an impromptu race up Boston harbor, and the pilots offered, without success, to pay the cost of drydocking so that they could examine her underwater lines.[16] The truth is that there was little under water to keep them from moving and apparently the woodboats never carried any ballast.

The lines in Figure 34 were taken from a later model which, unlike most woodboats, has a short counter. In comparison with Figure 33 this model has considerably more deadrise. The stem has much less curvature and no tumblehome, the bow is much less bluff, but there is the same long,

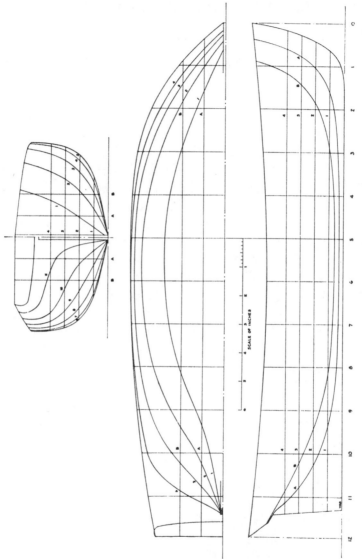

Figure 34. Lines of Saint John wood boat.

flat, easy run. There are indications in both sets of lines that the basic form was developed by the whole-molded process.

In keeping with their simple construction, the arrangements and fittings of the woodboats were also simple. The stem was not raised above the deck as on the Chebacco boats but prominent knights heads supported hawse blocks. On the typical boats there was an open rail at the bow and stern but none was fitted abreast the main hatch; on some of the boats of the 1830's there was no bow rail. Many of the later coastal boats were fitted with bulwarks about 30 inches high.

For years an iron anchor was a luxury that few woodboat owners could afford and a "killick" was commonly carried.[17] In one form this was simply a wooden anchor that required only three pieces of suitable material—a "Y" shaped limb of a stout tree, an oblong shaped flat rock, and a flat board of sufficient length to fasten to the arms of the "Y," and at right angles to the large stone that was placed in the crotch of the "Y". Two holes were made in the board to fit over the ends of the "Y" and it was secured by pegs driven through the protruding ends of the "Y".[18] The anchor cable was usually of hemp and for weighing anchor there was a log windlass worked by handspikes. It was generally located just abaft the foremast, which on the normal boats was stepped as far forward as possible on the stem knee, but occasionally the positions were reversed as on some of the Chebacco boats. As conditions changed iron anchors and chain cable became more common. The windlass in such cases was of the pump-brake type and the chain was often stowed in deck boxes port and starboard.

The mainmast of the woodboats was stepped just about amidships and the large rectangular main hatch was located just forward of it. A small hatch, usually located abaft the windlass, gave access to the fore peak. One or two log pumps were located between the mainmast and the cabin trunk aft. This cabin trunk was often quite prominent, particularly on the later boats where the quarters for the crew were entirely on deck. Entered through a companionway on the port side, the cabin was generally cramped and dingy with three berths and a brick fireplace that served for cooking and heating. Such fireplaces reportedly were used on woodboats long after stoves had come into general use on other craft. While most of the woodboats were steered with tillers, the later larger coastal boats were fitted with wheels. Boats operating on the Saint John River usually towed some sort of a tender, while the others carried a yawl boat on stern davits which often were of wood.

The average Saint John woodboat was too large to carry on the Chebacco boat practice of no shrouds or stays. They normally had a forestay to the stem, two shrouds per side on each mast, and a stay between the heads of the masts. Ratlines were not usually fitted — when the crew had to go aloft the mast hoops served. The two sails had long gaffs and were cut with but little peak; they commonly had two rows of reef points. For river work the rig of the average woodboat could be handled by a crew of two.[19]

The Saint John woodboats are now gone, but further to the north, working out of the little coves and harbors of Canada's Gaspé Peninsula into one of the roughest areas of the North Atlantic, are other descendants of the old colonial shallops. There are two versions, one employed along the so-called English Shore between the towns of Gaspé and Percé, while the other may be found along the southern coast on the Bay of Chaleur.[20] These waters were much frequented by New England fishermen in the late eighteenth and early nineteenth centuries.

A description of the hull of one of the English Shore

Gaspé boats is almost identical with that of a sharp-sterned Chebacco boat — only the pink aft is missing. She has a long, straight keel with considerable drag, a curved, raked stem, a straight, sharply raked sternpost, a straight rising floor, and a high, hard bilge. Instead of the practically vertical midship topsides of the Chebacco boat, however, those of the Gaspé boat flare out a bit. The bow and the lines in general are finer than those of the Chebacco boat. The dimensions and proportions of typical examples of the two types follow:

	Length	Breadth	Depth	L/B	D/B	Deadrise
Chebacco Boat						
1790	37.25 ft.	11.08 ft.	5.50 ft.	3.36	0.497	20°
Gaspé Boat						
1952	33.17 ft.	9.75 ft.	3.75 ft.	3.40	0.384	25°

Figure 35 is an outline comparison of the lines of these two vessels.

As for the arrangement, if a New England fisherman of 1790 could be put blindfolded aboard a Gaspé boat only two strange items would give him trouble. In the cuddy the brick fireplace would be missing and a small iron gadget would be giving off heat. In what normally would be the after fish hatch, there would be an oily-smelling roaring monster, for the Gaspé boats are now fitted with one- or two-cylinder gasoline engines.

While the stemhead of the Gaspé boat is not as prominent as on the old Chebacco boat it does have a heavy transverse pin and is employed as a mooring bitt. The Gaspé boat has the same raised cuddy deck forward with rails extending aft to the stern at its level. There are two standing rooms for fishing with fish hatches just abaft each. While the forward fishing room has a single fish hatch abaft it, the fish hold abaft the second fishing room is divided by the engine space on centerline and there are small hatches port and starboard. There is a third standing room aft for the helmsman.

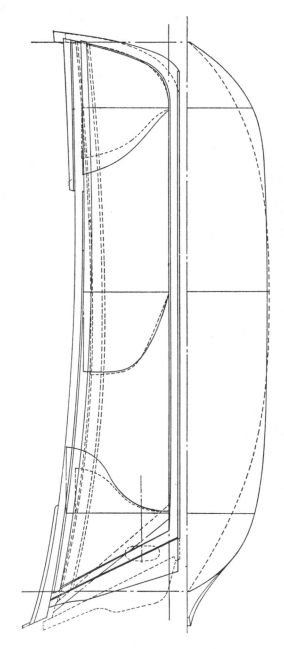

Figure 35. Comparison of Lines of Chebacco and Gaspe boats.

The Gaspé boats operating out of the Bay of Chaleur are similar to those of the English Shore but in general have more rake to their ends and there is some hollow to their garboards amidships. Their bilges are also hard but lower and their topsides have more flare. All the Gaspé boats are inexpensively built and construction is rough, the boats from the Bay of Chaleur being somewhat rougher than the English Shore boats. They are built of local woods — largely spruce, birch, and larch — with iron fastenings. Frames are steambent, often saplings run twice through a saw, and their heels are nailed to the top of the keel where they butt; floor timbers are not fitted. On the English Shore examples may be found of both carvel and clinker planking, with the latter more common, but practically all of the Bay of Chaleur boats have clinker planking.

The general practice has been to design the Gaspé boats as sailing craft and to adapt them for power by adding a false sternpost in which the propeller aperture is cut. As with the Saint John woodboats there is evidence of the use of the whole-molded process in the development of the lines.

It is in their rig that the Gaspé boats differ from the Chebacco boats for they are rigged as simple schooners with two pole masts and a short bowsprit secured on the cuddy deck to starboard of the stem. The standing rigging consists of a headstay, a pair of shrouds on each side for each mast, and a stay between the mast heads. For sails there are a staysail, a loose-footed gaff foresail, and a gaff mainsail fitted with a boom. There are no provisions for carrying topsails, indeed since the advent of power the trend has been to carry less sail and many boats do not use their foresails during most of the fishing season.

✿✿✿✿✿✿✿✿✿✿✿✿✿✿✿✿✿✿✿✿✿✿✿✿✿✿✿✿✿✿✿✿

CHAPTER VIII

Sloops 1700 - 1783

F OLLOWING the 560 named sloops in the Massachusetts Archives, the 70 sloops in the 1697 reports
of the county sheriffs of Maryland, and the 15 sloops also
reported in 1697 by Virginia's Governor Andros, there is a
considerable gap in the statistical and technical data concerning such craft although the quantity of pictorial information increases rapidly. The main body of colonial shipping
records for the eighteenth century prior to the American Revolution is missing, but there are enough bits and pieces to
indicate that during this period the sloop was the favored
type of small trading craft. The other types of small vessels
widely employed were the brigantine — often abbreviated
"brig" in the records so that we cannot always be certain of
its rig — and the schooner. The latter word, according to
oft-printed "tradition", first appeared about 1713 but we have
seen that what is now considered to be the schooner rig was
employed much earlier.

The following statistics gathered by Morris attest to
the popularity of the sloop:[1]

106

	Ships	Brigantines (or Brigs)	Snows	Schooners	Sloops	Others
1730 - Owned in Connecticut	-	3	-	2	37	-
1740-1758 Owned by Timothy Orne, Jr. of Salem	-	3	1	21	10	-
1762 Owned in Newport, R.I.	4	30	3	7	50	-
25 Sept. 1763 In port of Philadelphia	37	31	9	13	44	-
1776-1783 Connecticut privateers	10	51	2	51	88	56
	51	118	15	94	229	56

Concerning pictorial evidence, one of the best known sloops is that shown in the William Burgis 1729 view of Boston Light. This vessel actually was only incidental to the portrait of the lighthouse. Some sort of a beacon existed on Point Allerton in 1673 and Jaspar Dankers mentioned a lighthouse on a high island at the harbor entrance in 1680. Construction of a lighthouse on the present site was started in 1715 and the lantern was lighted for the first time on 14 September 1716. Three days later the following item appeared in the *Boston News-Letter*: "Boston. By virtue of an Act of Assembly made in the First Year of His Majesty's Reign, For Building and Maintaining a Light House upon the Great Brewster (called Beacon Island) at the Entrance of the Harbour of Boston, in order to prevent the loss of the Lives and Estates of His Majesty's Subjects; The said Light House has been built; and on Fryday last the 14th current the Light was kindled, which will be very useful for all Vessels going out and coming in to the Harbour of Boston, or any other Harbours in the Massachusetts Bay, for which all Mas-

Figure 36. Sloop off Boston Light, 1729. After Burgis.

ters shall pay the Receiver of Import, One Penny per Ton Inwards, and another Penny Outwards, except Coasters, who are to pay Two Shillings each at clearance Out, and all Fishing Vessels, Wood Sloops, etc. Five Shillings each by the Year."[2]

The special mention of wood sloops should be noticed for, along with fishing vessels, they were in and out of the harbor so often that they were assessed a yearly fee. Burgis's vessel, shown in Figure 36, is obviously no wood sloop and H. I. Chapelle considers that she is similar to the *Ferrett* class sloops built in England about 1711. One of these, *Hazard*, was sent from England to America in 1714 with the news of the accession of King George I to the throne and also orders for the colonial government. She was wrecked and lost off Cohasset, Massachusetts, on 12 November 1714.

The Burgis sloop shows many of the characteristics of the earlier New York sloops of the Duke's Plan and the Dankers sketch. Her loose-footed mainsail is of the short-gaff type with a long boom, and for headsails she has a stay-sail and jib; in light weather she probably carried a flying jib on the topmast stay as well. Although her standing yard is fitted with foot-ropes, the lower square sail may have been hoisted to the yard for setting, not furled upon the yard and let fall in the usual manner. A light square topsail would have been set flying on her topmast, which, it may be noted, is fidded abaft the head of the lower mast. The gaff-topsail was not widely employed until about the middle of the eighteenth century — early examples are shown on sloops and a schooner in a painting of a Maryland shipyard dated about 1760. An early Chesapeake Bay trading sloop with rigging similar to the Burgis vessel except for the square sails, Figure 37, has been redrawn from "A Platt of the Town & Port of Oxford," Maryland, dated 1707.

Figure 37. Chesapeake Bay sloop, 1707. After map by Turbutt.

Both of the famous views by William Burgis — New York in 1717 and Boston in 1725 — show large numbers of sloops of various hull and rig configurations. Some are open boats while others are decked and of a fairly large size. Many of the smaller sloops have only one headsail but the majority of the type have two. All sloops with boomed mainsails have short gaffs. Curiously, none of the New York sloops are fitted with yards although several are obviously naval vessels. Some of the Boston sloops are shown with yards and there are examples with furled sails having topsail yards aloft. Also absent from the New York view are any indications of Dutch influence in the form of leeboards. There is evidence that these fittings were employed, particularly on the shallow draft sloops that plied the upper reaches of the Hudson, until the early nineteenth century when centerboards were introduced.

The Roberts view of Charleston, South Carolina, of the late 1730's, the Heap view of Philadelphia of the early 1750's, and other representations before and after these dates too numerous to mention simply prove the universality of the sloop. To the seaman, however, there were small details which to him often told the home port and other information, as, for example, the description of a sloop found bottom up off Cape Cod in the autumn of 1729 — "Rhode Island built, with a blue Stern, two Cabbin Windows, her Counter painted yellow with two black ovals, and he thinks her sides were painted yellow, her Keel was about 40 feet, and her bottom Tallow'd. Her Counter had been Cork'd and Pey'd with Pitch over the Paint & not scrap'd off. Her Mouldings were all white. She had lost her mast, bowsprit and rudder."[4] Here was a hull at sea, upside down, yet the reporter could tell where it was built.

In general during the seventeenth and eighteenth centuries the design of large merchant ships followed that of similar sized naval ships and many small vessels aped the characteristics of the larger ones. In some localities, however, unusual conditions led to the development of various types of small, fast-sailing vessels. The Caribbean Sea, where buccaneers, privateers, and naval vessels from many countries cruised among the islands, was one of these. No vessel was safe from capture and if not large enough to fight off an attacker its safety lay in speed. In 1708 it was reported that the actions of French privateers had reduced the number of brigantines and sloops in Maryland to about a dozen in all, while Virginia had only six ships, eight brigantines, and two sloops.[5] Moderate sized fast vessels, capable of concealment in small harbors, were in demand and were supplied by shipbuilders on the various islands, particularly those of Jamaica, who developed a sharp-model sloop.

The principal characteristics of the Jamaica sloop were drag to the keel, considerable rise of floor, raking ends, low freeboard, and a raking mast. It had such a reputation for speed and weatherliness that orders for new sloops depleted the supplies of suitable timber on the island of Jamaica. Large numbers of the shipbuilders moved to Bermuda where the abundant growths of the light red cedar proved eminently suitable for the continued building of their specialty, which then became known as the "Bermuda sloop". The British Navy purchased or built sloops of this type for small cruisers and they were widely employed by the buccaneers, privateers, and traders.[6] Among the latter were the merchants of North America to whom, because of the British Acts of Trade and restrictions imposed by other European countries, the smuggling of rum, sugar, and molasses was a common and respectable occupation.[7]

Few plans of the Bermuda-type sloop have survived but the outline drawing, Figure 38, of the British naval sloop *Ferrett* of 1711, mentioned earlier, shows many of the features of the type. With a length on the gun deck of 65 feet 7 inches, she had a keel length of 50 feet, a breadth inside her planking of 20 feet 10 inches, and a depth of hold of 9

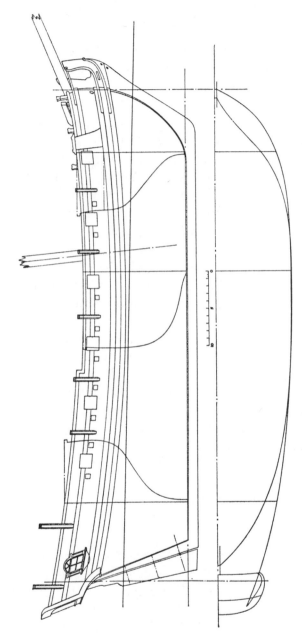

Figure 38. *H.M.S. Ferrett*, 1711. After Chapelle.

feet. Her burden was given variously as $113^{55}\!/_{94}$ and $117^{33}\!/_{94}$ tons. The outline of her midsection shows a moderate rise of floor with a slight hollow in the garboards, an easy bilge, and topsides that flare out slightly; the latter feature improves stability and does not restrict the room on deck for working the guns. The load water-line has a slight hollow forward and is relatively fine aft. Such a form goes far to dispel the delusion under which many labor that all old ships were chunky tubs and that hollow water-lines were invented during the clipper ship era of the mid-1800's. In company with most small vessels of her time, *Ferrett* could be propelled by sweeps in calms, there being ports for eight sweeps on each side.

We can assume, however, that an ordinary trading vessel sailing in less hazardous waters would not have needed the extreme characteristics of the Jamaica or Bermuda sloop. To substantiate this assumption Figure 39 shows the features of a British hoy of 1720. While the type name "hoy" was rarely used in North America, there certainly were many vessels performing the same service, for a hoy is defined by the Oxford Universal Dictionary as — "A small vessel, usually rigged as a sloop, and employed in carrying passengers and goods, particularly in short distances on the sea-coast". This hoy was very nearly the same size as *Ferrett*, having a length on deck of about 64 feet, a keel length for tonnage of about 47 feet 6 inches, and a breadth inside her planking of 19 feet 6 inches. Her midsection shows very little rise of floor, no hollow in the garboards, a very easy bilge, and considerable tumble-home to her curved topsides. Note that her load water-line forward is even fuller than *Ferrett*'s deck line.

Trade with Bermuda and the West Indies introduced the Jamaica or Bermuda sloop to the Chesapeake Bay region and during the first half of the eighteenth century Maryland

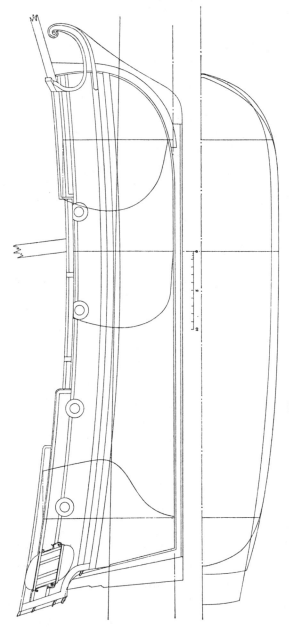

Figure 39. British hoy, ca. 1720.

and Virginian shipyards turned many sloops of the type. The problem of manning such large sloops led eventually to the use of the more easily handled schooner rig on the same type of hull, the result being, of course, the Baltimore Clipper. In the vessel registrations preserved in the Massachusetts Archives the home ports of many of the Massachusetts-built sloops were in the West Indies; hence it is very probable that they were constructed on the Bermuda model too. The oldest surviving plan of an American-built vessel is a sloop of the Bermuda type, *Mediator*, built in Virginia in 1741, whose basic features are shown in Figure 40.

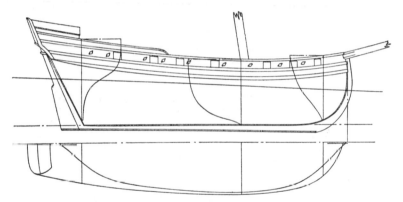

Figure 40. Virginia-built sloop *Mediator*, 1741-2. After Chapelle.

Although *Mediator* had one more gunport on each side than *Ferrett*, she was slightly smaller with a length on deck of 61 feet 4 inches. The length of her keel for tonnage was 44 feet, her breadth inside the planking at deck level 20 feet 11 inches, and her depth of hold 9 feet 9 inches; her tonnage was 104^{7}%$_{94}$ tons. *Mediator*'s midsection shows a similar hollow in the garboards, but her rise of floor is greater than *Ferrett*'s — 20° versus 14½°. The bilge has the same easy form, but there is more flare to the topsides. Her profile shows one feature of the Bermuda-type sloop missing in *Ferrett* but prominently shown on the many pictorial representations of the type — a short stern cabin with a highly crowned top.

The only known lines of a Bermuda sloop were published in 1768 by the great Swedish naval architect Fredrik Henrik af Chapman in his collection of ship plans titled *Architectura Navalis Mercatoria*. The plans in this work were gathered over a period of years from many sources. The original drawing for the engraving of this sloop was probably obtained in England between 1752 and 1757, but it may date from an earlier period, 1741 to 1744, when Chapman was working in English shipyards. The basic features of this Bermuda sloop are shown in Figure 41.

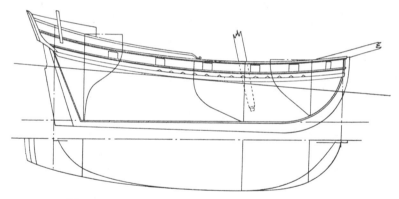

Figure 41. Bermuda sloop. After Chapman.

Of the same general size as *Ferrett*, the hoy, and *Mediator*, Chapman's Bermuda sloop had a length on deck of about 61 feet 3 inches. The length of her keel for tonnage was about 43 feet 6 inches and her breadth inside the planking 20 feet 4 inches. No structure is shown, hence it is not possible to give her depth of hold, but it was close to 8 feet. The sloop's profile shows much more drag to the keel than on *Ferrett* or *Mediator*, but she has a similar curved stem and a well raked sternpost. The stem profiles of the four sloops offer an interesting comparison, although the head structure on *Ferrett* and the hoy tend to divert the eye from the rabbet line which is the real shape of the hull. In relation to the line of the top of the keel, the rabbet line profile of this Bermuda sloop is nearly vertical at the bulwark level, an old form, while those of the other three tumble home considerably. The stem of *Ferrett* is less rounded at the bottom, which results in extreme hollows in the lower waterlines The great difference between these sloops lies in the shapes of their midsections — they show quite well the possible range. The hoy could have taken the ground between tides, if necessary, but the Bermuda sloop never could. In the midsection of the latter we find the direct evidence of the great rise of floor — here 25° — that was a feature of the Baltimore clipper schooners. There is no hollow in the garboards, the bilge is relatively hard and high, and the topsides are practically vertical. On Chapman's Bermuda sloop we again find the little stern cabin with its high-crowned top.

While sea-sloops — to differentiate them from those for local trade only — built on the Bermuda model were extremely popular with the merchants of the Chesapeake Bay region and very likely also with other colonial merchants to the north who conducted trading operations with the West Indies, we cannot assume that all colonial sea-sloops had its features. There certainly were many types of cargo which could not have been carried conveniently because of the extreme rise of floor and many waters where the nearly 12 foot-draft of the Chapman example would have been at a disadvantage. One such cargo was lumber, which before 1775 could by law only be imported by Great Britain from her North American colonies in sloops. For this trade there were

sloops even larger than *Ferrett* or *Mediator* — one of 140 tons
was built on the Kennebec River in Maine in 1772.[s] While
plans of these large lumber sloops are not available, there are
reasons for believing that they probably differed but little in
form from the many moderate-draft full-bodied sloops shown
by Chapman.

Unlike the Bermuda sloop and a few other special types,
the nationality of the majority of the vessels depicted in Chapman's collection is not given. In all cases, however, the plans
are of vessels with which he was familiar; hence we can
assume that the sloops shown were typical of those in the
Baltic and North Sea Trades. One of the other identified
vessels, however, was an English sloop built for the French
wine trade — a very burdensome sloop that had the hull form
characteristics of a large cargo ship. If certain details had
not been shown, one might assume that she was a much
larger vessel.

This wine sloop, Figure 42, had a length on deck of
about 58 feet, a keel length for tonnage of 43 feet 3 inches, a
breadth inside her planking of 17 feet 9 inches, and a depth
of hold of about 11 feet. Designed to sail with little drag to

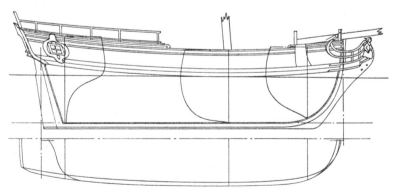

Figure 42. English sloop for the wine trade. After Chapman.

her keel, her draft forward was about 6 inches less than the 10 foot 3 inch maximum at the sternpost in contrast to the 3 foot 3 inch difference for Chapman's Bermuda sloop. The wine sloop's sections show a real "barrel-shaped" hull. The rise of floor of the midsection is about 7°, but the sraight floor is very short. It will be noted that the water-lines are very full at both ends, fuller even than those of the 1720 hoy. The sloop's weather deck has a rise of about one foot forward over her short forecastle and a similar rise to her quarter deck aft over her extensive accommodations, for she normally carried a few passengers in addition to her wine cargoes. It is probable that a large number of the North American sea-sloops of the eighteenth century that traded across the Atlantic prior to 1775 had hull forms similar to that of this wine sloop. Lumber and tobacco in casks were common eastbound cargoes while the sloops often returned with wine from Fayal and other ports.

Concerning the rig of the eighteenth-century sea-sloops, there seems to have been a fairly consistent combination of fore-and-aft and square sails. In the former category there were the mainsail, foresail, or what we today would call a staysail, jib, and flying jib — gaff topsails appeared after the middle of the century. For square sails there were the course, topsail, and sometimes a topgallant. In 1762 the 55-ton trading sloop *Prosperous Polly*, probably built in Rhode Island, had no topgallant sail, but the armed 50-ton British sloop *Edward* did in 1776; thus perhaps a tonnage of about 50 marked the limit for the fitting of this sail. These two sloops would have been about 46-47 feet long on deck. The smaller sloops intended for bay and river use where much tacking was necessary seem never to have had square sails.

We have noted that prints from the early eighteenth century show that when fore-and-aft mainsails were fitted with booms they had short gaffs. When furled such a sail was not secured to the boom but first to the gaff, which was then hoisted part way up the mast, and the remainder of the sail made up in a long roll out to the end of the boom. The foresail or staysail was often shown furled in stops along its stay while the jib was furled on the bowsprit. We have also noted that fore-and-aft mainsails with long gaffs were fitted on yachts and other craft in the second half of the seventeenth century. These mainsails were invariably boomless and as the gaffs — more commonly called half-sprits — were standing spars such sails were furled by brailing into the mast. There are but few examples of these long-gaff boomless sails in early North American views.

A seemingly logical step would have been to increase the area of the boomed mainsail by fitting a long gaff. This took considerable time but it appears to have been accomplished by the mid 1700's. Sail plans or spar dimensions from which a sail plan could be reconstructed are not available for *Ferrett* or the 1720 hoy but, in view of the print evidence, we can assume that a least *Ferrett* had a boomed mainsail with a short gaff. From the rake of her mast, it is possible that the hoy did, too, although hoys of her day were commonly fitted with the long standing gaff that developed from their earlier spritsails.

On the other hand, spar dimensions for both *Mediator* and Chapman's Bermuda sloop are available. A reconstructed sail plan of *Mediator* by H. I. Chapelle was published in the United States National Museum Bulletin 219 — *The National Watercraft Collection* — and it shows a loose-footed boomed mainsail with a long gaff. Figure 43 is a reconstruction of the sail plan of Chapman's Bermuda sloop from her spar dimensions — she also had a long gaff. In both cases the gaffs are about nine-twentieths of the lengths

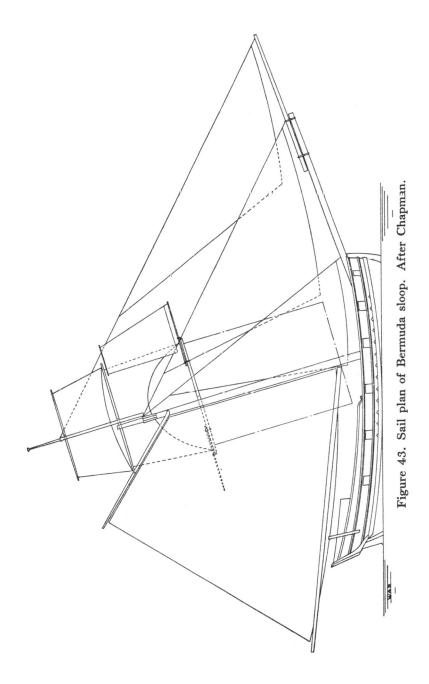

Figure 43. Sail plan of Bermuda sloop. After Chapman.

of their respective booms. Judging from one of a series of rigging sketches that Chapman included in his book, the English wine sloop would have had the same sails as the Bermuda sloop without, however, as much rake to her mast. This rigging sketch and any number of prints show that on large sloops mainsails normally had three rows of reef points, foresails two, and jibs one; no reefs were shown on the square sails.

Every yachtsman knows that boats accumulate all sorts of miscellaneous gear. Starting with a clean boat in the spring and taking practically nothing on board during the summer he finds that by fall lay-up time there are several carloads of equipment to be removed. By contrast, apart from personal items and food, the inventories of some of the eighteenth-century sloops illustrate the fringe conditions under which many of them operated. Excluding spars and sails the following equipment was on board the 55-ton sloop *Polly* in 1762:[9]

> "Two anchors two cables Two boyes with their Ropes
> A Binnicle & two Compasses
> Two half hour Glasses
> Two Pumps, Three Speers & Six Pump Boxes & Two
>   Pump hooks
> A Cambooze Two Iron Pots and a Saddle
> Four Iron Bound Water Caskes of Sixty Gallons Each
> Two Wooden bound Do. of One Hundred Gallons Each
> Two Axes, Two hammers, and Chisell and Drawing
>   knife
> two Gimletts two Calking Irons one hand Saw
> A Hand-line and lead
> An Ensign, a Parcell of Old Iron"

But there were no spare sails, no canvas for repairs, and no spare rope, all items that one might expect to find on a vessel in service. Some vessels did carry a few such spares, but it was not unusual to find that a sail had to be cut to provide patches for a more necessary working sail.

In describing vessels carrying a single-masted fore-and-aft rig with headsails, the works of many yachting writers from the last quarter of the nineteenth century on to the present have given rise to many misconceptions. I refer to the seemingly endless arguments as to the difference between a cutter and a sloop. In light of the eighteenth-century sloops that we have been discussing, some clarification as to the origins of the cutter may not be amiss as the term first appeared around the middle of the eighteenth century. I am sure that whatever I may write will have little effect on the present day concepts, for, as with many other types, the period in time is so important.

Blanckley in his MS *A Naval Expositor* of 1732 did not include the term cutter; his unique definition of a sloop has already been quoted. *The Oxford Universal Dictionary* dates the first nautical use of cutter as 1745 when it was — "A boat, belonging to a ship of war, shorter and in proportion broader than the barge or pinnace, fitted for rowing or sailing, and used for carrying light stores, passengers, etc." — but the H.M.S. *Wager*, a sixth-rate in Anson's fleet that sailed to the South Seas in 1740, had such a cutter.[10] The dictionary's second definition is — "A small, single-masted vessel, clinker- or carvel-built, furnished with a straight running bowsprit, and rigged much like a sloop, as a *revenue cutter* c. 1762".

A 1784 British Act for the prevention of smuggling indicated that by that time a fixed bowsprit was one of the identifying marks of a sloop. It also showed that cutters then had running bowsprits, but that, other than this feature, there was no distinctive cutter rig. Along with other small craft, cutters then had clinker planking, an indication of light construction.[11]

The 1815 edition of Falconer's *Marine Dictionary*, which is mainly an expansion of the first edition of 1769, stated that a sloop was — " a small vessel furnished with one mast, the main-sail of which is attached to a gaff above, to the mast on its foremost edge, and to a boom below, by which it is occasionally shifted to either quarter. It differs from a cutter by having a fixed steeving bowsprit and a jib-stay; nor are the sails generally so large in proportion to the size of the vessel." The definition of a cutter in this work is — "a small vessel commonly navigated in the English Channel, furnished with one mast, and a straight running bowsprit, that could be run in on deck occasionally; except which, and the largeness of their sails, they are rigged much like sloops. Many of these vessels are used on an illicit trade, and others employed by the government to seize them. . . ".

Lescallier in his *Traite Pratique de Gréement des Vaisseaux* noted, however, that form had some bearing on the difference between sloops and cutters. The hulls of cutters were built with more depth than those of sloops and, operating with less freeboard, their greater draft enabled them to carry sail better. Cutters were rigged like sloops, but differed in that their masts raked aft, their spars were longer, and their sail area greater. While normally carrying the same sails as a sloop, a cutter could usually set a ringtail on its mainsail in addition — this was a sort of bonnet set between the gaff and the boom along the after edge of the mainsail. Cutters were considered to be fine sailers. Sloops were sometimes armed and employed as privateers, but for this purpose they had to be specially built for sailing and were then called cutters.

The running bowsprit of the cutter meant that the jib,

the flying jib, too, if carried, had to be set flying instead of on a fixed stay. Apparently because of this difficulty Chapman drew his cutter with only a foresail and a jib while the sloop had three headsails, but the total sail area of the cutter in relation to the hull profile was greater than that of the sloop. Essentially, then, the cutter originally was a lightly-built sloop-rigged vessel destined mainly for employment by smugglers or those seeking to apprehend them, as privateers, or for light naval duties, and for such uses it carried a greater sail area than a merchant sloop of the same size.

CHAPTER IX

After The Revolution

W E HAVE noted that at the close of the American
Revolution in 1783 the impoverished condition of
the new nation's fishermen, who were mainly New England-
ers, led to a boom in the building of Chebacco boats, this type
being a development through the earlier two-mast boat of
the colonial shallop. The term shallop, however, was employed in Massachusetts at least as late as 1806. During the
war years there were occasional items such as the following
from the *Boston Gazette* for Monday, 25 August 1777 — "No-
tice is hereby given, That libels are filed before me against
the following Vessels, their Cargoes and Appurtanances, viz.
. . . In behalf of John Vincent and others against the shallop
called the *Relief*, of about 10 tons burthen, Samuel Norwood,
late Master. . .". This shallop and other vessels were seized
for furnishing supplies to British ships off the coast.

Other references from the previously mentioned Diary
of the Reverend Mr. Bentley of Salem indicate that in his day
shallops were still employed for fishing. In his entry for 5
April 1792 he noted — "That morning arrived a shallop from
the Bay, out 48 hours, which brought in several hundred fish,
& were in the act of preparing them for the flakes".[1] There

is a further reference to what is probably a fishing shallop on 21 August 1806.[2]

In view of the earlier material on the Saint John wood-boat and the Gaspé boat, Bentley's reference to the people of Nova Scotia on 19 April 1797 is interesting — "The roads of the interiour country are bad, so that few of them have any tolerable accounts of the distance by land, & their Shallops always furnish them with a ready means by sea, & they have excellent harbours on all their coasts".[3] On 20 September 1798 he reported that some Salem men — "who left this port for the Spanish Main in a Shallop, have foundered at sea. Their vessel was deep & small, & they had an heavy gale upon leaving port".[4]

The exact type of boat referred to by the newspaper accounts and Bentley's notes is probably lost in time. From the various entries in his Diary it is apparent that Bentley was well acquainted with various types of boats and vessels, as who in Salem was not in those days; hence there seems to be little danger of mistaken identity. He does not, however, specifically mention a "two-mast boat". Three of his entries concerning shallops came before his first entry concerning Chebacco boats; yet the fourth is seven years after. Considering conditions during the war years and the state of the fishing fleet after the war when the government bounties were offered, it is quite possible that a few old square-rigged shallops were repaired and put into service. There is no pictorial evidence for the late survival of such a boat, but we can hardly expect any artist to have been interested in portraying an outmoded type.

Although these late references to shallops in Massachusetts and Nova Scotia raise some questions, there are no doubts about the use of shallops on the Delaware River, for they were still common on that river in the early decades of

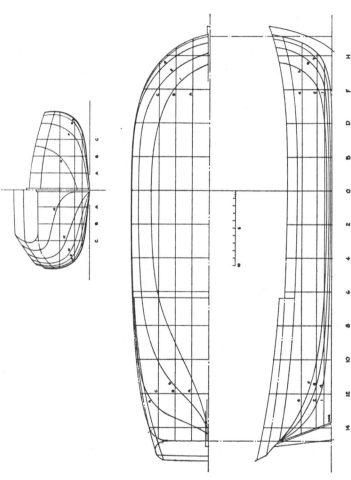

Figure 44. Delaware River shallop, 1818. After Humphreys.

the nineteenth century. The Reverend Mr. Bentley, however, when seeing a Delaware River shallop for the first time, would undoubtedly have described the vessel as a sloop, which for all practical purposes it was. The well-known Durham boat — rowed, poled, and sometimes sailed — carried loads of 15 to 50 tons on the upper Delaware, while the shallop was the common general freight boat of the lower river and its major tributaries.[5] The lines of a Delaware River shallop of 1818 are shown in Figure 44; they have been redrawn from a plan in The National Archives by Samuel Humphreys, the famous designer of many of the early vessels of the United States Navy. This shallop was a shoal-draft keel vessel having a bluff bow and a square stern. Her length was 54 feet, her breadth 21 feet, and her depth only 4 feet 4 inches. Like most small vessels of the period she had a raised quarter-deck beneath which were the crew's accommodations.

The mast of a typical Delaware River shallop was located well forward and was supported by two shrouds per side and a single headstay to a short bowsprit. There were normally but two sails — mainsail and jib. Shallops employed on the Schuylkill River, where bridges barred normal passage, had their masts stepped in tabernacles, Dutch-fashion, so that they could be lowered. A painting by John James Barralet dated about 1805, depicting a shallop with its mast down, does not seem to show any shrouds.[6] A shallop's usual crew apparently numbered three, two of whom could be employed at sweeps in calms, working around wharves, and passing bridges. A typical shallop based on a painting by Thomas Birch is shown in Figure 45.

In Maryland and Virginia shallops and even small sloops were seldom mentioned after the middle of the eighteenth century. The shallops were outmoded while the small sloops were probably taken for granted. There was, how-

Figure 45. Delaware River shallop, ca. 1820. After Birch.

ever, an increasing use of small schooners (some as small as 20 feet on the keel) of the burdensome, simply-constructed flats", and of log canoes. In the absence of trained boat builders the early Virginians adopted the native dugout and quickly improved it by sharpening the ends. Although among the early inhabitants of Maryland there were competent boat builders, a change in the economy of its Eastern Shore about the beginning of the eighteenth century, caused by a shift from the growing of tobacco to the production of linens and woolens, changed the local shipping requirements. The log canoe then proved useful for fishing, oystering, and other pursuits. Outgrowing the simple, hollowed-out log, the canoes were later built of from two to five logs; the ultimate in log construction was the well-known bugeye.[7]

In addition to the sad state of its fisheries in 1783 the new American nation found that it had practically no merchant marine suitable for foreign commerce; the majority of its vessels were coasters or ex-privateers. Instead of being able to send fleets to Europe as had been predicted, vessels from Great Britain, France, and other countries glutted the markets with goods of every description but mainly the luxuries that had been unavailable for seven years. Even after the signing of the peace treaty on 3 September 1783 shipping and shipbuilding remained in the doldrums as the price of independence had included the closing of the British West Indies ports to American traders; France and Spain, but recently allies, did the same. Although not large markets, the Danish, Dutch, and Swedish islands remained open and were good centers for smuggling.

By 1786 the exports of Virginia were higher than their pre-war figures as they were items, chiefly tobacco, much in demand in Europe. The exports of Massachusetts, however, were only a quarter of what they had been twelve years earlier. Conditions slowly improved as France and Spain soon permitted direct trade with their West Indian possessions, and there were many schemes by which New England's main commodity, salt fish, found its way to the British West Indies to be exchanged for return cargoes of rum, sugar, and molasses.[8]

In spite of the depressed conditions some enterprising

American merchants sent their vessels further afield and there were some notable voyages in sloops. In December 1783 the 55-ton Hingham sloop *Harriet*, Captain Hallet, sailed from Boston to China with a cargo of ginseng root; because of its aromatic and stimulant properties this root was greatly esteemed in China. Calling in at the Cape of Good Hope, as was the custom, for provisions, water, and wood, Captain Hallet found a returning fleet of British East Indiamen. Alarmed by this introduction of competition the captains offered him two pounds of Hyson tea for each pound of ginseng root. Hallet accepted and returned to Boston having made a very profitable voyage.[9]

By accepting this trade Captain Hallet lost the opportunity of being the first to hoist the American ensign in Canton. This honor went to the ship *Empress of China*. She sailed from New York on 22 February 1784 and returned 14 months and 22 days later. Other vessels followed her route arolnd the Cape of Good Hope including the 80-ton Albany-built sloop *Enterprise* under the command of Captain Stewart Dean. With a crew of seven men and two boys she sailed from New York on 15 December 1785 and returned the following year.[10]

The 90-ton sloop *Washington*, Captain Gray, sailed from Boston on 30 September 1787 in company with the 212-ton ship *Columbia*, Captain Kendrick, bound for the Northwest Coast of America; they were the first recorded North American vessels to double Cape Horn. The story of the *Columbia*'s second voyage in 1792 with Gray in command and the discovery of the river that bears her name is well known. *Washington* crossed the Pacific several times and was lost in 1793 in the Straits of Malacca; in the latter part of her career she was re-rigged as a brigantine.[11]

Perhaps the most ambitious of the sloop voyages was that begun in 1794 by the 98-ton *Union* under the command of the 21 year old John Boit, Jr. According to his journal — "The sloop *Union* was fitted out in Newport, R.I., for a voyage to the North West coast of America, China, Isle of France and back to Boston. She was completely overhauled during the months of July and August, and on the 28th of August dropped into Coasters Harbor. Stores and provisions were taken aboard for a three year's cruise, besides a cargo of sheet copper, bar iron, blue cloth, blankets, trinkets, and other articles suitable for traffic with the North West Indians for furs. The sloop was completely fitted out for the voyage with a crew of 22 in number. Had good quarters, mounting 10-carriage guns, 6 & 3 pounders & eight swivels on the rails".[12] On the sloop's return to Boston on 8 July 1796, which completed the first and probably only circumnavigation of the world by a sloop until modern times, the following was one newspaper's complete account of the voyage — "Sloop, *Union*, Boit, Canton".[13]

Regarding *Union*'s performance Captain Boit wrote the following — "She proved to be an excellent seaboat, and was a very safe vessel. Still I think it too great a risque to trust to one mast on such a long voyage, when a small brig would answer on the N. W. Coast as well . . . No vessel that left Canton in company with the *Union* made so quick a passage, although we were detained a fortnight at the Isle of France. She rarely exceeded 130 knots a day, though once northbound in the Pacific with a strong wind abeam and following sea, fine weather, under all sail she logged 168 and 188 knots for two consecutive days".[14]

Union's portrait, Figure 46, based upon Captain Boit's drawings in his journal, shows several differences from the earlier large sloops. Her hull had the typical head structure

Figure 46. Sloop *Union*, 1795. After Boit.

and quarter galleries of a large vessel. The little stern cabin with its highly crowned top was no longer in favor — in its place was a long raised quarter deck. Four windows per side forward of the quarter galleries indicated relatively extensive accommodations below this deck. Basically *Union* carried the same assortment of fore-and-aft and square sails as had the earlier sloops. Her flying jib stay, however, led from the outer end of the jib-boom to the lower mast head instead of to the topmast, and apparently her topgallant was set flying. Instead of having reef points both her foresail and jib were fitted with bonnets and each had two sheets — a single line from the clew of the bonnet and a purchase from the main body of the sail. Her square topsail had a single row of reef points.

Even in *Union*'s day, however, the large sloops were being replaced for overseas voyages by the more easily handled schooners for certain trades and by brigs for others. The rerigging of *Washington* has been mentioned and Captain

Boit's comment on single-masted vessel has been quoted. Sloops did remain strong in the various river and coastwise services; the latter included voyages to the West Indies. As late as 1836 sloops were still employed in the New Bedford-West Indies trade, for in that year the sloop *Benjamin Franklin* was built in Huntington, Long Island, to carry cattle out and molasses home. She was 65 feet long with a breadth of 21 feet. Although designed as a coastwise vessel, she ended her days on the Hudson River; she came to the river before 1864 and sailed until 1889 when she became a lighter in New York harbor.[15]

Since the arrival of the first settlers at its mouth, the Hudson or North River has been an important artery of commerce; because of the configuration of its bank the river has often been called the American Rhine. From the early days sloops were employed on the river carrying passengers and freight between the various ports along the nearly 160-mile stretch from New York to Troy. In the nineteenth century, as steamboats improved and railroads stretched up the river along each shore, passenger traffic dwindled but sloops carried freight on the North River until the 1890's. The service was unusual in the large numbers of passengers carried and in the extent to which hull shape and rig were adapted to the demands of the traffic and sailing conditions on the river. In 1771 there were 125 sloops operating on the river and by 1810 the number had grown to 206.[16]

Until 4 March 1814 vessels on the Hudson and those operating in the country's other river and coastwise passenger and freight services, while generally operating on definite routes between certain ports, had not sailed at any particular time. On that date New York newspapers carried what is probably the first published announcement in America of a line of packets pledged to sail on a definite schedule. The advertisement for the "New Line for Albany," which was founded by a group of New York and Albany merchants, read in part — "The Subscribers being duly aware of the advantages that would arise to shippers of Goods and Produce between Albany and New York, by having a Line of Sloops formed to ply between the two places, to sail on set days, have therefore purchased three of the first rate Sloops, viz. the *Gold Hunter*, to be sailed by Capt. Martin, the *George*, Capt. Ostrander, and the *Hardware*, Capt. Weller. One to sail from Albany every Saturday, and one to sail from New York every Saturday, and one of which will be in New York ready to receive freight at all times, as she will arrive before the other leaves".[17]

The often published plans and photographs of models of the justly famous large centerboard sloops, such as *Victorine* of 1848, leads one to believe that all North River packet sloops were of this type, continuing the tradition of the shoal-draft Dutch sloops with leeboards, and that, except for an occasional oddity like *Benjamin Franklin*, no other type existed. There is ample evidence, however, that a large number of the early nineteenth-century North River sloops — " . . . were very sharp, much deadrise, deep keel with great draught of water. . . " and drew much more water aft than forward; this is not unlike the description of the Jamaica or Bermuda sloop. Such sloops operated very successfully on the lower reaches of the river but it is known that *Benjamin Franklin* for a time carried coal from Rondout Creek.[18]

One of the famous keel sloops on the North River was the long-lived *Illinois* of Newburgh, built in 1818 and lost off Point Judith in 1890. Measuring about 150 tons she was 84 feet long with a breadth of 26 feet and a draft of 12 feet. Originally built as a passenger packet *Illinois* — ". . . had a cabin about half the length of the vessel for the accomodation of passengers, two after-cabins or state-rooms, altogether in both cabins some twenty-six or twenty-eight berths. The cabin was built of hard wood, much of it mahogany, with a very large oval mirror across the bulkhead, separating the main cabin from the state-rooms aft. . . . She had a very long companion-way, with large brass signal lamp hanging in the centre for light at night, and a floor of hard wood, kept very white and clean. . . . What was termed the forecastle, the place set aside for culinary purposes, was arranged much after the manner of the houses of that day, having a chimney and fireplace of brick, also a mantel over the fireplace, and a brick hearth in order to keep the vessel from fire. There were four berths also in the forecastle for the accommodation of the men in the vessel".[19]

As was customary in her day *Illinois* carried but three sails — mainsail, a single headsail called the jib, and a gaff topsail. The masts of the river sloops were located well forward making the mainsails relatively much larger than on seagoing sloops. While two or three headsails were no problem on the latter, they were a nuisance on the river sloops that had to track frequently and quite early the single headsail became standard on them. There are several fairly large sloops so rigged in the background of the 1717 view of New York. Compared with seagoing sloops the total sail area of those on the river was relatively much larger in order to make use of the lightest of breezes. The relatively greater breadths of the river sloops, however, made them very able and in fresh winds taking in the topsail was usually a sufficient reduction of sail. It was customary to reef the mainsail in thunder squalls; this was done by lowering the sail the necessary amount and securing the luff and leech only. Reef points were seldom used as lazy jacks kept the sail controlled along the boom.[20]

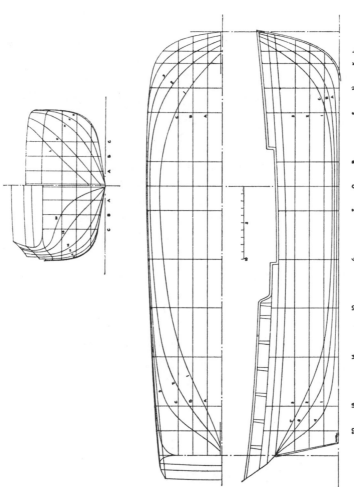

Figure 47. Sloop, ca. 1838. After L. McKay.

At this point two interesting hold-overs from the early days are worth mentioning. *The Sloops of the Hudson* by Verplanck and Collyer contains lists of 355 sloops and 123 schooners, some of the latter converted from sloops, that sailed on the river. In the list of sloops are two vessels carrying what was then called the "periauger" rig, two masts with gaff sails and no headsail — the old two-masted sloop. An historical society in a small New England town where sloops, Chebacco boats, and schooners were known for years owns a model of a small decked vessel carrying the same rig that bears the label — "Captain ——'s first fishing sloop".

Redrawn from Lauchlan McKay's *The Practical Shipbuilder* of 1839, Figure 47 shows the form of a shoal-draft keel sloop of the 1830's. McKay considered that she — ". . . is a good model for speed and burthen, and has width to enable her to carry from 70 to 75 feet mast, according to the waters she may be required to navigate. If for a coasting vessel, the former would be quite sufficient, and if for river freighting, the latter may even be increased. . .".[21]

On Chesapeake Bay by 1820 there were shoal-draft sloops similar in form to the famous Norfolk pilot schooners. They had plain curved stems, little or no overhang aft, no bulwarks, and few deck structures. For sails they had only a gaff mainsail and a jib; they carried little or no standing rigging. Probably originated by fitting a sloop rig on a small schooner hull, the type in 1820 had less draft than the pilot schooner; while leeboards were often fitted, some sloops had centerboards. A typical centerboard sloop then was about 55 feet in length with a breadth of 20 feet; its centerboard was about 16 feet long.[22]

The introduction into western naval architecture, that of Europe and North America, of what we now call a "centerboard" had a profound effect on the design of shoal-draft ves-

sels, for prior to that time it was next to impossible to build
such vessels that could work well to windward. Leeboards
as employed in the Netherlands were, of course, a solution to
the problem. In North America they were used on the above
mentioned Chesapeake Bay sloops, on vessels around New
York and on the Hudson River, on a few scattered scow types,
and occasionally on Great Lakes vessels. This introduction
is generally credited to Captain John Shank, R.N., in 1774
while stationed in Boston. "In consequence of a hint from his
Grace the Duke of Northumberland," he constructed a small
boat with a "sliding keel". Having a length about three-quarters of that of the boat this "sliding keel" worked vertically
through a watertight case or trunk and when lowered by
tackles at each end it projected a short distance below the keel
of the boat. Because this long trunk was objectionable Shank
later employed two or three "drop keels" as they came to be
called. The British Admiralty built several brigs and ship-
sloops as long as 113 feet with drop keels, but leaky trunks
eventually discouraged their use. Drop keels had been employed before Shank's time by the Chinese on their junks and
in South America on various types of sailing rafts.[23]

The first authentic record of a board working on a pin is
a model — perhaps still in existence in Ipswich, England —
made by Mr. Molyneux Shuldham, R.N., in 1809 while a
prisoner of war at Verdun.[24] In the United States a patent
was issued in 1811 to three brothers named Swain of Cape
May, New Jersey, for a "lee board through the bottom"
pivoted on a bolt near its forward end and lifted into its watertight case by a lanyard or tackle at its after end. It was said
that the first boat of any size in the United States to be fitted
with such a device was the sloop *Advance* built in 1815 at
Nyack, New York, by Henry Gesnor; yet another authority
stated that the first on the Hudson River was in the sloop

Freedom built by Cornelius Carman.[25] Needless to say, the use of the centerboard spread rapidly to coasting and river sloops and schooners; it was even fitted in large three-masted schooners where the main mast was stepped off-center in way of the trunk.

❀❀❀❀❀❀❀❀❀❀❀❀❀❀❀❀❀❀❀❀❀❀❀❀❀❀❀❀❀❀❀

CHAPTER X

The Packet Sloop Mayflower

ON
NORTH RIVER
BETWEEN 1678 & 1871
MORE THAN 1000 VESSELS OF FROM 30 TO 470 TONS WERE BUILT
OF THESE IN 1772 ICHABOD THOMAS CONSTRUCTED THE SHIP
BEDFORD AND THE BRIG BEAVER. THE FORMER WAS THE FIRST
VESSEL TO DISPLAY THE UNITED STATES FLAG IN EUROPEAN
WATERS OFF TRINITY ENGLAND FEB. 6, 1783. THE LATTER
WAS ONE OF THE FAMOUS TEA SHIPS OF BOSTON HARBOR
THE SHIP COLUMBIA 212 TONS
MOUNTING 10 GUNS BUILT BY JAMES BRIGGS IN 1773 WAS THE
FIRST U. S. VESSEL TO CIRCUMNAVIGATE THE GLOBE
IN 1792 HER CAPTAIN ROBERT GRAY DISCOVERED
THE COLUMBIA RIVER AND IT WAS
FROM THIS VESSEL THAT THE RIVER
RECEIVED ITS NAME

S O READS a bronze plaque on the rail of a bridge in Plymouth County, Massachusetts, between the towns of Hanover and Pembroke. How many more than the thousand vessels will never be known, for as mentioned earlier, the records for a large part of the eighteenth century have disappeared and in all probability many small vessels were never listed. This is known to be the case for the existing

records prior to 1715 when fishing vessels were not registered. The first existing record of shipbuilding on the North
River was in 1678 and included in that year's output was the
16-ton round-sterned open sloop *Desire*, but vessels were built
on the river at least as early as 1645. The last launching of a
major vessel was in 1871 when the 90-ton schooner *Helen
M. Foster* slid into the river from the Chittenden yard.[1]

The modern traveler who may have crossed bridges
spanning other rivers such as the Kennebec at Bath, Maine,
the Weymouth Fore River at Quincy, Massachusetts, and
the James at Newport News, Virginia, is quite aware of the
adjacent large modern yards for the building of steel ships.
He can hardly visualize, however, even the most productive
of the many yards for the building of wooden vessels that once
were located along the banks of the North River. For such
a yard, a plot of firm soil on the river's bank provided the required site. The total plant was probably no more than a
shed or two. Piles of logs and planks from nearby sawmills
were the raw materials which were fashioned into vessels by
workmen employing only hand tools — axes, adzes, augers,
chisels, mauls, and saws.

Standing today on the North River Bridge and looking
to the northeast downstream, one can view the sites of thirteen
former shipyards, two on the right bank and eleven on the
left. The northern abutment of the bridge covers most of the
way locations of two of the earliest yards. Between this portion of the river and Massachusetts Bay — seven miles as the
crow flies but eighteen around the bends — are the sites of at
least twelve other shipyards. Some sites seem to have been
used for about 25 to 30 years by one family while others had
a succession of builders for nearly 200 years.

The majority of the vessels built on the banks of the
North River had no claim to such fame as that attached to

Bedford, *Beaver*, and *Columbia* mentioned on the plaque. One whose name comes to mind whenever whaling disasters are mentioned was the ship *Essex* which was stove in by a whale in the South Pacific in 1819; she was built on the river in 1796.[2] The others were but the common working vessels of their times, some serving on overseas routes, but many more remaining in local waters employed in fishing and freighting. Only one steamboat was built on the river, the 21-ton *Mattakees* in 1839 to serve as a towboat, but the river was too crooked to permit the use of a proper towline and she was soon sold in Boston.[3]

A perusal of the list of vessels built on the North River shows many names derived from Greek and Roman mythology. Other vessels were named after prominent persons or perhaps one of their owners, but most had just plain country names. *Sally* was borne by fifteen vessels while *Mary* and *Betsey* were carved on fourteen each; *Polly* and *Hannah* were also popular. *Industry* served for nine vessels followed by *America*, *Hopewell*, and *Union* at eight each. As might be expected in Plymouth County, *Mayflower* was not forgotten and seven sloops, schooners, or brigantines bore that name.

One of the best ways of viewing the old North River shipyard sites is from the river itself. If we were to embark in a skiff or canoe — somehow the river does not now seem suitable for anything much larger — and row or paddle downstream from the bridge between Hanover and Pembroke, we would come around the third bend to the Pembroke Town Landing where there were once brick kilns and at various times two shipyards. This site may also be approached by land over Brick Kiln Lane. The earliest recorded shipbuilding at a Brick Kilns Yard was by Captain Benjamin Turner in 1730; the first recorded by name was the brig *Norfolk*

built by Ichabod Thomas in 1765. Shipbuilding at the Brick
Kilns ceased in 1850.[4]

The Francis Russell Hart Nautical Museum of the
Massachusetts Institute of Technology has two builder's half
models that are identified only to the extent that they came
from the Briggs yard at the Brick Kilns. From the above it
is obvious that they must be for vessels constructed prior to
1850. After some preliminary investigations the smaller of
the two, representing a relatively wide, shallow vessel, perhaps a sloop, seemed to offer the better chance of identifica-
tion. In view of the comparatively few known sloop models
it was considered to be worth the effort. The lines taken from
this model are shown in Figure 48. With a full bow and a full
stern, the vessel would have been no speedster but one well
suited for carrying freight in shallow waters.

The over-all length of the model is 24⅞ inches, its width
represents a total breadth of 8⅜ inches, and its minimum
depth is 2⅝ inches. The four bottom lifts are one-half inch
thick. Taking a clue from the thickness of these lifts and
assuming the model to have been built on a scale of one-half
inch to the foot, it was possible to make a few reasonable
assumptions and calculate the probable tonnage of the vessel represented. It can be stated that investigations based on
scales of three-eights and three-fourths inch to the foot led
nowhere.

In the United States the tonnage of a vessel operating
between the years 1789 and 1864 was calculated by the formula (L-3/5B) x B x D/95. Essentially this was the old
British rule introduced over a century earlier. As mentioned
in a previous chapter, older rules had employed the actual
keel length of a vessel, but as this was impossible to measure
once a vessel was afloat, the value (L-3/5B) was used. This
approximated the keel length for a considerable period of

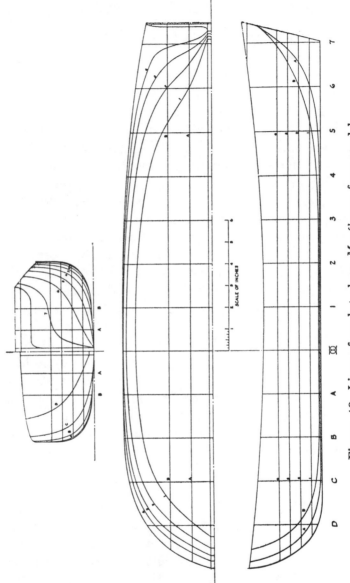

Figure 48. Lines of packet sloop *Mayflower* from model.

time. The length L was measured above the deck from the fore part of the main stem to the after side of the sternpost. The breadth B was taken at the broadest part above the wales to the outside of the planking. D, the depth, was taken as ½B for two-decked vessels, but for those with a single deck it was measured from the underside of the deck plank to the top of the ceiling in the hold.[5]

First considering the breadth of the model and of the vessel, 8⅜ inches equalled 16 feet 9 inches, and assuming this to have been the molded breadth, *i.e.* to the outside of the frames, two thicknesses of, say, 1¾-inch planking gave a total breadth B for the tonnage of the vessel of 17 feet ½ inch. For the length L, with no overhang aft to confuse matters, 24⅞ inches equalled 49 feet 9 inches, to which had to be added, say, 6 inches to the fore part of the main stem for a total of 50 feet 3 inches. The value of (L-3/5B) in decimals was then 40.03 feet. The depth for tonnage was more of a problem. From the molded depth at side taken from the model, there had to be deducted the depth of the floor timbers and the thickness of the ceiling while the camber of the deck had to be added. The model's depth of 2⅝ inches represented 5 feet 3 inches, and allowing 12 inches for bottom structure and 4 inches for camber, the resulting depth for tonnage was 4 feet 7 inches. The tonnage of the vessel was then 40.03 x 17.04 x 4.58/95 or 32⁸⁴⁄₉₅.

The family name of Briggs was associated with shipbuilding from the early days in Scituate and members of the family moved from there to other locations along North River. At least three of the family built ships at the Brick Kilns - Seth, his son Elisha, and his grandson Luther. Luther Briggs, who was born in 1784 and died in 1854, built in 1823 one of the seven recorded *Mayflowers* constructed in North River yards, a packet sloop of 32⁴⁴⁄₉₅ tons.[6] Her enrollment in Plymouth, Massachusetts, dated 7 June 1828 gives the following information:[7]

> *Mayflower*, sloop   Port of hail - Marshfield, Mass.
> Built at - Pembroke, Mass.
> Tonnage - 32   Length - 49'-9" Breadth - 17 1/24'
> Depth 4'-7"
> One deck, one mast, square stern, no galleries, no figurehead.
> Master - Asa Sherman
> Owners - Asa Sherman, Elisha Phillips, Stephen Rogers, Jonathan Stetson, Jesse Reed, and Chandler Sampson of Marshfield; Alden Briggs, Elias Magoun, Horace Collamore, Gilman Collamore, and David Magoun of Pembroke; Elisha Foster, Jr. and Elisha Tolman of Scituate.
> Master Carpenter - Luther Briggs
> Surveyor - John B. Barstow

Considering the inevitable minor variations that occur in stepping up from a model to a full-sized vessel, the model and vessel dimensions are remarkably close. It can be assumed with little doubt that the model represents the sloop *Mayflower* of 1823.

Fourteen owners may seem a lot for one small sloop, but such multiple ownerships were common. Packet sloops such as this *Mayflower* served to connect the North River communities with Boston and other points along the coast and they were jointly owned by the business men of these communities. Asa Sherman, *Mayflower*'s master, skippered North River packets for many years; *Nancy*, a 94-ton schooner built at Scituate Harbor in 1803, was one of his earlier packets. His son, Asa, Jr., commanded packets for thirty-seven years from 1827 to 1864.[8]

The down-river cargoes of the packets included cord

wood, charcoal, and farm produce. The full cargo of the sloop *Ranger* in 1733 from North River to Plymouth was three barrels of cider.[9]   On return trips the packets brought goods for stores, sawn lumber, and various supplies for the shipyards.   There were eight regularly served landings along the river, some of which are not now easily accessible.   The first from the sea was at White's Ferry, near the present bridge, to Humarock Bridge over the *South* River.   To a person viewing the North and South Rivers today this may seem like a strange detour, but during the entire period of shipbuilding along its banks, the North River took a right-angled turn as it approached the sea and flowed south behind Humarock Beach for a distance of about three miles before joining the South River and turning eastward into the sea.   The present mouth of the river was opened during the great *Portland* Storm of 1898.

The second landing was at Little's Bridge, formerly Doggett's Ferry and now the crossing of Route 3A.   Union Bridge, formerly Oakman's Ferry, was the third followed by Hobart's, Foster's, and Job's Landings.   Then came the Brick Kilns and finally the Hanover Town Landing at North River Bridge.[10]

The sloop *Mayflower* served as a North River packet until July 1828 when she was sold to the Watson family of Plymouth.   At this time Asa Sherman took command of the new packet sloop *Magnolia* of $36^{17}/_{95}$ tons, which was a few inches larger than *Mayflower* in all dimensions.

Except for the small wedge fairing the deck line at the stern, the result of the top lift having been not quite thick enough, the lines of *Mayflower* in Figure 48 are as taken from the model. It is interesting to compare her lines with those of the Delaware River shallop, Figure 44, as both vessels were intended to carry large loads on limited drafts.

Mayflower was proportionately slightly narrower and deeper than the shallop and had less rise of floor. *Mayflower* probably did not have a centerboard — it would not have been of much use in the river where progress in one direction or the other depended to a considerable extent on the tides. The first North River packet sloop known to have had a centerboard was the 47-ton *Hanson* built by Luther Briggs and Barker Turner at the Brick Kilns in 1833 and commanded by Asa Sherman, Jr. She was described as being very heavy and very flat on the bottom; her rise of floor was only three inches.[11]

Mayflower's profile, deck plan, and sail plan, Figures 49 and 50, are reconstructions based on the general practice of her day. Several possible variations were considered and discarded. For example, she might have had a raised quarter deck. Such a feature was mentioned in many vessel enrollments, but not invariably included. The bulwark at the stern might have been raked aft above the deck, supported by heavy knees, to enclose the head of the rudder. Considering the vessel's service this seemed like a needless refinement so the rudder was left entirely outboard as on the Saint John woodboats.

Looking at *Mayflower*'s arrangement, her bowsprit is stepped in a single bit post which holds the pawl for her log windlass that is worked by handspikes. An access hatch to the forepeak is just abaft the windlass. Following the rules, her mast is stepped three-tenths of her length from the bow. Her main cargo hatch is just about amidships and just forward of her trunk cabin are two log pumps. Considering the windings of the channel in North River it seemed better to show a tiller rather than a wheel.

The standing rigging is simplicity itself—three shrouds per side and a headstay. For sails there are the mainsail,

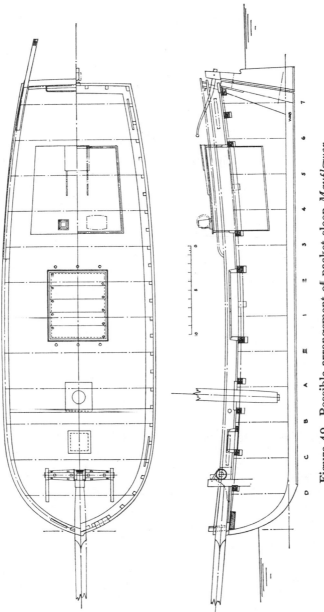

Figure 49. Possible arrangement of packet sloop *Mayflower*.

Figure 50. Possible sail plan of packet sloop *Mayflower*.

still loose-footed, and the jib. The light topmast may be un-
warranted, but it could serve to spread a light topsail that
would be useful on certain reaches of the river. The river
banks in *Mayflower*'s day were undoubtedly far less wooded
than today so there might not have been as much blanketing
as one might imagine.